# 08:46

Fresh Perspectives

# 08:46

Fresh Perspectives



ISBN 9798746388704

*PUBLISHED BY*

New World Theatre Publishing
Londonderry, NH
newworldtheatre.org

## TABLE OF CONTENTS


| | | |
|---|---|---|
| | FOREWORD<br>By LeLand Gantt | iv |
| | INTRODUCTION | vi |
| | PERFORMANCE RIGHTS | vi |
| **MONOLOGUE** | **PLAYWRIGHT** | |
| What Are You Going To Do | LeLand Gantt | 1 |
| UnRhythmic Slave | Karen L Smith | 3 |
| Michael is Black | Michael Hagins | 4 |
| November 4, 1967 | Melda Beaty | 7 |
| Your Grandma Was Out There | Christopher Buchanan | 9 |
| Tired | Shaneisha Dodson | 12 |
| Define "Black" | Nessa Amherst | 13 |
| A Sickening Loop | Tina Fakhrid-Deen | 16 |
| I AM NOT YOUR TEACHER | Kayodè Șoyemi | 17 |
| Walk a Mile in My Rage | Gary Earl Ross | 26 |
| HashtagTheBlackGirl | Cashel Campbell | 27 |
| to kneel or not to kneel | Bryan-Keyth Wilson | 30 |
| Why I was late today, and will probably always be late as a Black woman. | Liz Morgan | 32 |

TABLE OF CONTENTS


| MONOLOGUE | PLAYWRIGHT | |
|---|---|---|
| How Dare You?! | Jonathon Benjamin | 36 |
| LOST GENERATION | SIRI IMANI | 37 |
| Inertia | James J. Johnson | 40 |
| Red Card | Michael Rishawn | 44 |
| Outer Inner Monologue | Louis DeVaughn Nelson | 45 |
| A Gathering of Old Men | Gladys W. Muturi | 50 |
| It's Over, Queen Mya | Sharece M. Sellem | 51 |
| UNBECOMING TRAGEDY | T. R. Riggins | 53 |
| When It Rains | J. J. Tingling | 57 |
| The Sleeping Cop | Max King Cap | 58 |
| Black by Unpopular Demand | K. E. Mullins | 61 |
| FIRESTORM | Antonio David Lyons | 66 |
| The Reapers on Woodbrook Avenue | Mardee Bennett | 68 |
| The Signing | Sharon Cleveland Blount | 69 |
| Epicenter | Zachariah Ezer | 72 |
| reconstructing whiteness | Alva Rogers | 74 |
| Antigone's Monologue | Marie Mayingi | 78 |
| The Voice Inside My Head | Louis D. Johnson | 79 |

| MONOLOGUE | PLAYWRIGHT | |
|---|---|---|
| SPIT | Diana Mucci | 82 |
| I Didn't Raise My Son To Die | Sharnell Blevins | 88 |
| A Park For Children To Pretend In | Vincent Terrell Durham | 90 |
| Follow the Fireflies | Christian St. Croix | 91 |
| Monologue for a Tutting Face | J. E. Robinson | 94 |
| The Last Days or The Meek Shall Inherit the Earth | Ardencie Hall-Karambe, PhD | 96 |
| Drawing While Black | Maurice Moore | 100 |
| Certain Aspects of Conflict in the Negro Family | Tylie Shider | 107 |
| I'm tired | Rachel Lynett | 108 |
| Create the Space | Cris Eli Blak | 111 |
| Mother to Son | Crystal D. Mayo | 113 |
| Happy Birthday | Dr. Mary E. Weems | 116 |
| KNOCK | Rajendra Ramoon Maharaj | 119 |
| BIOS | APPENDIX A | 124 |
| CONTACT INFORMATION | APPENDIX B | 144 |

**FOREWORD**

"THE MURDER OF GEORGE FLOYD" That's where all this started. I wonder if that will be history's headline. The eight-minute-and-forty-six-second moment of Derek Chauvin's nonchalant knee on George Floyd's neck? When I saw the video, it took *my* breath away; caught me up like a bug trapped in amber. I walked around for days in a numbed-out frozen fog.

Until I saw the video of the young woman who had captured the event on her cell phone. Asked how she felt about what she saw, she said, "How do you think I feel?" I thought: "This young black woman was Chauvin's second victim that day. Whatever her life could have been, whatever semblance of innocence she had living in today's world, was gone forever—stolen by witnessing this heinous act, committed with such arrogant impunity right in front of her, AND tasked by fate to record it!" I thought on how many others would suffer from the destructive energy emanating from that act, like concentric circles of sonar, infecting the psyche, inflicting terror, conveying a corrosive worthlessness. I thought on the hundreds of years of reiterated patterns: our voices choked from our bodies, our bodies choked from this life, our historical narratives—if not erased—corrupted.

And I got pissed. Frankly? I went "elemental." I felt like a barely contained volcano. A tsunami of murderous rage, impelling me to violence, threatened to overwhelm me. I was literally vibrating, in danger of bursting at the seams. I wasn't numb anymore. I was on fire, ready to erupt.

Now. Here's the "Matrix" moment. You know, "Don't ask me to explain." Was it "The Ancestors?" My "Guardian Angel?" Or, is it just what artists do? All I know is, gripped by a nearly uncontrollable urge to destroy something, I somehow managed to sit down at my computer and channel all that rage onto the page. I called the piece "The Fire This Time?"— riffing on Jimmy Baldwin's title. I wrote about my rising blood lust and my vulnerability to its siren call. I posted my scream on Facebook; I submitted it to the New York Times. And I felt a slow release of toxic pressure. The fire still raged, but now that I'd "caught my breath," I had agency, control of the bellows, of myself and my narrative. I wouldn't succumb to the knee-jerk spasm of rage fueled violence, adding to the statistical narrative of just another incarcerated or dead black man. I would continue to breathe and use that breath to power my voice—written or spoken—to reflect a perspective on this world, illuminating a reality that may seem alien to some—and for that reason, all the more necessary to be expressed.

That's when the call came inviting me to contribute to and help curate this anthology of BIPOC voices. Artists of like minds, all. Soulful, fantastical, courageous voices, irradiating the pain, pride, depth, richness, beauty and scope of this American BIPOC reality. Voices brimming with the vitality of veracity—slapping that *GONG* of truth—shattering that ancient framework of mendacity, creating new and invigorating narratives. I am honored and humbled to have been instrumental in helping to create a platform upon which these fabulously talented, incredibly inspirational artists can stand and share their voices with the world.

I invite you to listen and experience the power of perspective.

**LeLand Gantt**
Collection Curator
Contributing Playwright

**INTRODUCTION**

In the wake of the murder of George Floyd by the former Minneapolis police officer, Derek Chauvin, on May 25, 2020, the collective members of New World Theatre agreed we had to speak out and take action. As writers, we marshaled our words into a public Statement of Conscience, which we and others signed. We also declared our commitment to action, vowing to seek out and actively engage with playwrights of color to broaden our understanding and encourage and support works that express a fuller range of the human experience.

It is an honor to publish such wonderfully diverse, powerful voices from the Black community of playwrights. As you read these collective works, you will discover beauty, tragedy, humor, resilience, and strong words that challenge us to broaden our perspective.

Our collective future hinges on a better understanding of those outside the small cloistered spheres we inhabit, and we hope this book will help to shatter those barriers that too often keep us apart.

**PERFORMANCE RIGHTS**

Performance rights and royalty license agreements must be obtained when any of the works within this anthology are performed before a paying audience.

For those seeking to perform all the monologues within this collection, contact New World Theatre to obtain a royalty license agreement for *08:46*.

For those seeking to perform one or more of the monologues within this collection, but not all of them, contact the individual playwright to obtain a royalty license agreement.

Playwright contact information is available in APPENDIX B.

# 08:46

Fresh Perspectives

# WHAT ARE YOU GOING TO DO

By LeLand Gantt

Yeah. But you did nothing.

This is a hard truth to tell, let alone hear. No. You aren't racist. Per se. But you have been steeped in it all of your life. If racism were a teabag, you've been swimming around, fish-like, in its water since the day you were born. Yes. We both have. But YOU have benefited, albeit, unconsciously, from this racist system—you, your parents, their parents—ignoring the existence of any other reality, while that very reality stares you in the face every day. Your delivery person, your nanny, your dental hygienist. Your gardener, your super, your doorman. That homeless person (of color? Do you even really notice?) you step over every day on your way to work. Or the gym. Or lunch.

You are complicit. Because you did nothing. No. YOU weren't the grocery market cashier demanding ID from that black woman to cash her check, but you didn't ask said cashier why she didn't ask you for yours.

And, hey. I get it. It's NOT your reality. Living while white isn't a bonus or a privilege; it's NORMAL. Everyday. White folk can, and often do, walk down the street like they are the only ones there, oblivious to me and people who look like me. Even when some KNOW me, they have to kind of "psycho-emotionally separate me from the herd" before acknowledging that fact. To themselves. And, again, I get it. Context is everything. Why SHOULD you recognize me outside of our shared context, the specific place in your consciousness where you see me, where I have your permission to exist? The "death of a thousand cuts" from daily micro-aggressions, so unintentionally hurtful, delivered so casually, don't concern you because you don't experience them. "Officer Timson" is your friend. Your blood pressure doesn't spike or your anus clench when he turns his attention your way.

And, of course, what you can't see can't hurt you. Right? Wait a sec while I confer with that Ostrich after I pull what's left of him—his head—out of that hole. Out of sight, out of mind. Hear no evil, see no evil, speak no evil. Pick your monkey. I get it. Not your problem. Not in your wheelhouse. Not your purview. You don't see us, you don't hear us, you haven't felt any need to advocate for us.

And so, you did nothing.

After Oscar. And Trayvon. And Sean. And Walter. And Eric. And Amadou. And Tamir. And Breonna. And Michael. And Sandra. And Freddie. And Antwon. And Edward. And Ahmaud.

And . . .

And you did nothing.

And now George. And that sound like popping bubble wrap you hear is the surprised/terrified jerking of a world full of heads out of a world full of holes. Well, DAMN! Do you see us now? Do you hear us NOW? After George? And, listen. I'm not gonna look a gift horse in the mouth. To be seen is a wonderful thing. I'll take it. But. What does it mean? Now that you see me, what now? And WHY? WHY do you see me? I think that is a very important question. For my continued optimism; my aspirations for survival. Is it because you finally saw us in George? Pinned face down, damn near under a car, by three "overseers", one with a knee on his neck? Or is it because you finally saw YOURSELVES reflected so nonchalantly in that "thug's" eyes. Hand in your pocket. Kneeling for Jesus. For almost nine minutes. Or did you see yourself in one of the others; not actually choking him, just keeping him down, or acting as sentry to impede any interference?

Did you see you?

Did you finally see the truth for what it is? That you are, have been, complicit? Because you did nothing?

And here we are. On the cusp of . . . SOMETHING.

Yet again.

And.

What are you going to do?

# UNRHYTHMIC SLAVE

By Karen L Smith

The Un-Rhythmic Slave Everyone sees yet only the BLOOD-SUCKERS engage Drowning your Queendom with mass destruction supporting your menace to society Reframing you from the SPIRITUAL RHYTHMS

The Un-Rhythmic Slave

A society that once stolen you from the Mother Land A society that forced you on a ship striped you from your future of leadership Brain-washed your hopes and dreams dousing your family tree with repeated less than, hopelessness, darkness even when light appears

The Un-Rhythmic Slave

Centuries passed but not hatred not the attacks on "The Changers" the poison still spreads 20th and 21st centuries SLAVE SHIPS delivering crystals (crack) to control the masses, the educated, the intellectual, political reps, the un-assuming, the insecure, the curious...THE REJECTED!

The Un-Rhythmic Slave

She continues to wander the streets... Day or Night, the Un-Rhythmic Slave Beaten by her past, present and possible future Dis-respected by neighbors, black sheep of the family hunted by the BLOOD-SUCKERS Can't hear the DRUM...Can't feel her RICH LEGACIES... Focused only on self-destruction.... Focused on the next hit... Til THE INVISIBLE NOOSE snaps...her neck...

# MICHAEL IS BLACK

By Michael Hagins

**MICHAEL:** The first time I ever realized I was Black was in the 8th grade. I remember watching two students fight in the hall of high school. I was confused why they were fighting, and I heard the people chanting... the n-bomb. I mean... chanting it. The other Black students began to push and shove and it turned into this huge fight. I ended up getting thrown into lockers and getting knocked out. It was more embarrassing than painful. Only one white student got detention. For a day. For the Black students the decree handed down from the administration was simple: any fighting would result in 10 day suspension or worse. When I told my parents what happened, my mother shook her head and told me, "Don't ever get into a fight in that school. They'll throw you out and give that other little cracker a cookie."

I learned two valuable lessons that day: learn from your mistakes, and keep your head down.

*BLACK nods and smiles in approval.*

This is a section of my story. There's a lot of stories that need to be told. And here is part of mine. Normally a white guy plays this part for me, because it's safer when a white man speaks in an angry tone of voice. When a Black person is angry... well, we know how that usually turns out... but today... we're in a safe space, so my friend will speak for me. I'm still a little afraid to speak for myself. Don't worry... he's a better actor than me. I mean... I'm a better actor than... you get the idea.

I went to a performing arts college, because theatre was the one thing that made me feel like I was a part of something and for once my race and my awkwardness wouldn't be a factor. So, my third day of class in college I went up to do a monologue for an audition for a Shakespearean play called Love's Labour's Lost. I felt so strong and so powerful at the time. Turns out that all this time when I was thinking I had real emotion and commitment, no one could understand what the fuck I was saying. My dream of being an actor turned to complete shit in one critique. I never got over that one day... when I was told I talk too fast. I've been trying to get over that for years... seriously... YEARS. It's not over yet either. As you can see... I STILL have anxiety about it.

I also had a stutter. My mother told me, "I couldn't match all the words in my head to my mouth." So, I read four different speech books; one by Edith Skinner called Speak With Distinction. I studied the IPA every single day. I hit my plosives with a hammer. I hit my vowels like crazy. I did everything I could to be a better actor and to be understood. And for all that hard work I got Ferdinand Pillar, a major part in Vaclav Havel's play The Memorandum. And I should note that Ferdinand Pillar is the colored mute in the play.

*MICHAEL takes a card from off-camera.*

... apparently I also speak like a white person. I was told that several times by several people, both Black and white. I never was able to fit in even with my own race. And because of that, it made me ashamed to... speak in public. I've been told: I "talk like a white man," I "walk like a white man," sometimes even "act like a white man." Why talk for myself? Why not have a white man just talk for me? Maybe they'll hear me now! It makes me self-conscious. It's scary. Imagine wanting to be in a business where rule one is being understood and you have to say things twice and you feel shame about your voice. You feel ashamed because you don't sound like a certain race. You talk too fast. You stutter. You can never say anything with confidence. You hate every single thing about your voice, and you can do nothing about it. And you're supposed to be an actor. The vast ironies of life.

Some people hear me, some even try to understand me. But they can't. You know what makes it really hard are those white people who tell me "they get it." They grew up poor, they grew up afraid of the police, they grew up being criticized. They go through the same things I do. No, you don't. You don't know what it's like. At all. YOU'RE. NOT. BLACK. You don't tense up passing a police station. You don't hold your breath in the subway. You don't cry watching the news. You don't get tired of every single protest and argument asking for some kind of reform met with anger and vitriol. Or maybe you do get tired. Maybe you're tired of hearing about the death of another Black person, maybe you're tired of hearing about a rapist getting away with it, maybe you're tired of hearing a person with a trans identity just want to be themselves. Fine... be tired. You're tired of it... maybe some of us are living with it. And living with it directly. So don't try to understand. Maybe help us? Maybe fight for us? And maybe shut up for once and listen. Maybe help us be able to speak out without consequences or judgement? Eh... what do I know? I'm just a dumb Black guy who's still afraid to speak for himself.

You know, we should lighten this up. Maybe we should change the subject. Something a little different. (to BLACK) OH! We haven't talked about religion yet!

*BLACK looks at him quizzically.*

Come on. If we're going to reveal this much religion and politics are huge.

*BLACK hates this but passes him a card.*

I'm agnostic.

*MICHAEL looks for more.*

(speaking as the actor) That's it?! What about politics?

*BLACK thinks hard, then writes a long time on a card, thinks about it, then passes him a card.*

I'm Black. (as the actor) Oh, come on!

Who's been there for me? My friends. I have them. I admit there are times I feel lonely, but I'm not alone. It gets scary sometimes, but in the end, I have to maintain hope. I have to stay positive.

# NOVEMBER 4, 1967

By Melda Beaty

**CARRIE:** (forty years of anger and pain collide) Alberta Mae Johnson as long as you squat to pee, don't you ever use blaming and Ricky's name in the same sentence. You don't know nothing about Ricky's death, cause you were too busy running back and forth to Chicago which yo' fake furs and yo' men folk. You weren't here when they came on this here porch at two in the morning. You weren't here when they kicked my door down with they mangy dogs looking fuh Ricky. Wouldn't even let me open my own door and invite them in proper. They pushed past me with them dogs and their guns pointed right at my face. Those police dragged my son out of his bed in nothing but his drawls. I kept telling them 'Suh, he ain't done nothing. He ain't done nothing, suh.' Ricky screamed 'mama... mama,' but they just kept pushing and kicking him down these steps, and when he was too weak to stand, they drug him by his arms along the concrete. They threw my boy in the back of that police car like they was taking out the trash.

I called every police station in Quitman County, but I couldn't find Ricky fuh three days. Fuh three days, he sat in a cold jail cell with no clothes, no lawyer, wouldn't even let him make a phone call. Nothing. And fuh three days nobody had the sense enough to call me. When I finally got to see him, they had kicked him in his ribs so many times; he couldn't even sit up straight. His eyes were swollen to the size of plums. Lips bigger than his whole face. Police say somebody saw Ricky robbing a white woman's house in Clarksdale. That's what they said, Alberta. They said. I sat through all them trials. Nobody there but me and a sea of white folks and their fancy lawyers and all-white jury. So that judge gave him twenty-five years to life. The lawyer they gave Ricky was as crooked as a dog's hind leg. Couldn't afford no good one, so I wrote letters to everyone I could think of to help get my boy out of that jail 'cause God as my witness, he ain't robbed nobody! He wasn't raised that way.

(breathes)

So, I wrote letters every day and not one response. Then I wrote every week, and then every month, and finally every year, and no one, not the mayor, the pastor, the governor of Mississippi, not even the president of the United States even bothered to help me!

(breaks)

But November 4th, 1967, Sheriff Turner banged on my door to tell me that they found Ricky's body hanging in his cell wearing nothing but his drawls. Said he committed suicide, but he didn't. They killed him, Alberta. They killed my seventeen-year-old son for a crime he didn't do. So, excuse me, if I ain't ready to dance a jig about Obama or anything this world has to offer.

# YOUR GRANDMA WAS OUT THERE

By Christopher Buchanan
(Excerpt from *Angels Watching From Afar*)

*PATRICIA, black, 70s, grandmother of two and retired nurse. Stoic and faithful, she is woman of pride, well accomplished, but weathered in her life experiences and set in her ways. She is determined to protect her family ... at all costs.*

*February, 2017. A living room in a house in Washington, DC.*

**PATRICIA:** I got a two-by-four in that closet over there. You talk to me like that again, it's gonna go right across that fat mouth of yours. Now, don't you get it twisted, little girl, I am with the cause. One hundred percent. But this is a battle we've been fighting since this country's inception and if you're gonna fight it, you best know what you're up against. Now, you sit your black ass down right now and listen to what I have to say! (pause)

I was out there. Ohhhh, yes, your grandma was out there. I remember when I visited my grandpa in the hospital. Holy Cross it was. Cancer was eating his body away, so I went down to visit him for the last time. Got to the front desk and asked security to see him. Guard stone told me "No. You're wearin' pants." Back in those days, they could turn away a gal for wearing slacks. Bet you didn't know that with your young feminist self. So, I says to him "hold that thought." I took a couple steps from that desk and dropped them trousers right then and there. Folded them up just as neat as could be, draped them over my left arm, went right back up to that desk, looked that man dead in the eye and said, "Excuse me. I'd like to see my grandpa." Hmph. You shoulda seen that man's jaw drop the floor! He pointed me straight to grandpa's room.

So, pop-pop tries to talk, but couldn't. Lungs were filled with fluid, so he wrote some parting advice on a piece of paper ... "Fight for what's right, but walk away when you can. Don't let no man take your breath away." He knew I had formed this group with some high school friends ... Mikey, Mae and Charlotte. We were the

Petworth Freedom Riders and, child, we were some serious bad asses! We antagonized cops with protests right there at their precincts.

We went to the big marches, too. I was just 23 when we saw King give his "I Had A Dream" speech and for the first time in our lives, we felt some real, tangible hope. But five years later, all that hope was gone when King got shot. There was a People's Drug Store over on 14th and U and news of his death was blaring on their radio. There were about 30 of us in there, including Stokely Carmichael, and he said "Well, if we must die, we better die fighting back." But, he changed his tune real quick as the crowds started shouting ... "Let's burn these stores down! Let's go kill us some honkeys!" Stokely was arguing with these youths, tellin' them to go home, calm down and fight another day. But ain't no one listened. Including me. "Stand up for Martin! Stand up for Martin!" we chanted. Over and over again, we chanted.

A mustang pulls up and we think it's undercover, but turned out to be one of Stokely's friends. And one of the finest revolutionaries of our time hopped in that car and got outta dodge. "That nigga is fake," we said, "Let's take these streets!" So, we start throwing rocks, bottles ... we lootin' and burnin' stores! DC police made an about face! But, Johnson calls in the National Guard and they came in with the tanks and the heavy artillery. Bullets are flying. Bones crackin'. Blood spillin' and bodies are dropping like flies! We start running and broke into this place ... Lord, I forget the name, but they were a carry out that was well known for their fried chicken and mumbo sauce. We revolutionaries were hungry! Anyway, we're eating and next thing we know, a raging fire breaks out.

We dumped them wings and high-tail ourselves out that building ... or, so we thought. Mikey never made it out. Took authorities two days to find his remains. Had to cremate him 'cause he was already burned so badly. And you know what happened at his funeral? I found grandpa's piece of paper right there in my coat pocket.

Unfurled it, read those immortal words and realized how badly I failed.

Over eleven hundred fires burned that night. Burned down damn near half the city! And for what? So cops can shoot us down like boars in the wild? So we can be harassed, beaten and raped by these dirty, no good, entitled men? So, we can send a white supremacist to the highest office in the land? Huh? What's changed? Nothing. Not in the five hundred years we been in this God forsaken land and it damn sure won't change 'cause the two of you say so. So, you think about that the next time you wanna go risking your lives, 'cause some silly hashtag ain't gonna stop a cop from blowing you away. I had to bury Mikey and I just buried your parents, so I ain't burying the two of you!

# TIRED

By Shaneisha Dodson

Being a black woman is one of God's most precious gifts. It's also one of the toughest because we are forced to carry everyone's weight on our shoulders. Black women are tired.

Tired of being ignored. Tired of being devalued. Tired of being disrespected. Tired of being the most unprotected species in the world. Tired of crying our eyes out every time one of us is murdered by the same people who have been sworn to protect us. Tired of being blamed for our own death. Tired of seeing our sons, brothers, uncles and loved ones being reduced to nothing but a hashtag. #RestInPeace

Tired of fighting for our place in this world that only acknowledges us when it's trendy. Black lives matter. All black lives matter. All life matters. My life matters. My life has always mattered. Tired of chanting to deaf ears.

Tired of fearing for my own safety. The anxiety is unbearable. My fears are constantly living rent free in my head. Haunting every second of my day. I don't feel safe in my home. I don't feel safe in my bed. I don't feel safe jogging. I don't feel safe driving. The thought of me being suffocated for eight minutes and 46 seconds is exhausting. I'm sick and tired of being tired. What more can I do?

# DEFINE "BLACK"

By Nessa Amherst

"Why do you talk like that?"
"You dress like you're white."
"You like classical music?!"
"You don't like fried chicken?!"
"You don't like BET?!"
"You're not black."

For the love of God, please shut the hell up!

I'm sorry if I'm not your definition of what "black" is supposed to be. But I happen to like who I am, and I wouldn't change it for anything.

I enunciate because my mother taught me to do so, just as her parents taught her and her siblings. Slang wasn't an option. It still isn't, come to think of it.

I enjoy shopping at mainstream stores like LOFT, Old Navy, Stitch Fix, and more because I want to feel beautiful.

I don't eat fried chicken or any fatty foods because it is unhealthy for me, and I'm trying to sever ties with diabetes and bad heart health in my family.

I enjoy ALL types of music - classical, jazz, Latin, Broadway, oldies, rock, alternative, Tin Pan Alley, old school R&B, etc. because of my upbringing and musical education.

I enjoy watching sitcoms, period dramas, anime, Disney movies, films from the Golden Age of Hollywood, animal programs, home decor shows, and Saturday morning cartoons because it makes me happy and relax.

Is there really supposed to be a general representation of what "black" people should be?
I don't think so.
I hate to break this to you, but what you see on TV and film doesn't even come close to what ALL blacks are.

As a matter of fact, that's called stereotyping.
And it needs to stop.

For example...

I'm not a gangster or drug addict.
I don't drink alcohol.
I don't smoke cigarettes or marijuana.
I don't go around dropping f-bombs or other curse vocabulary every second word when I talk. (I don't do anything of that because it makes me uncomfortable.)
I don't limit my music experience to just black artists.
I don't go to clubs on weekends or any given night.
I'm not a loud-mouth.
I don't do any of those things Hollywood or the media paints us to be.

Here's a thought: Tell stories about the blacks you DON'T know about or see on a regular basis.

What about blacks who like anime?
What about blacks who like to exercise?
What about blacks who enjoy eating healthy?
What about blacks who like games like Dungeons & Dragons or Settlers of Catan?
What about blacks who are quiet and introspective?
What about blacks who are gay, lesbian, or transgender?
What about blacks who are mathematicians?
What about blacks who love the theatre?
What about blacks who speak other languages, not just Spanish because it's easy?
What about blacks who are scientists?
What about blacks who are paramedics, as well as doctors?
What about blacks who hold major roles in the armed forces?
What about blacks who are into Shakespeare?
What about blacks who enjoy traveling?
What about blacks who play in symphonies?
What about blacks who don't look "black"?
What about blacks who like classic novels by Tolkien, Jane Austen, or F Scott Fitzgerald, just to name a few?

What about blacks who love fantasy?
What about blacks who adore Disney movies?

Where are those stories?

Sometimes people ask me what I believe in as a black woman.
I believe that being black means moving forward instead of blaming the color of our skin for all of the problems in our country or in the world.
It means that we learn from our ancestors who fought for acceptance and equality, not chastise them for not doing enough.
It means embracing the things that makes us happy, even if it's things or ideas that are not so common for black people to do.
It means not following the crowd, and being proud of being your own person.
It means fighting for change that is long overdue, and not just doing nothing.
It means teaching others that character is far more important than color.

I was once told to "enjoy living on my plantation" because of my thinking that our ancestors wouldn't want us to live in the past but instead move forward.
For many years, that statement hurt me because of my progressive thinking.
But my progressive thinking has become my strength.

Our fight is far from over
But we shouldn't have to accept the stereotype of what our race is. Because that's not who we ALL are.
We deserve an equal representation of ALL the different personalities, likes, dislikes, and tastes.
Not just a small fraction because it's what sells or what is expected to be seen.

I'm not a perfect representation of what "black" looks like.
But I would rather be myself than be a copy of something that I'm not.

And that's the way it should be.

# A SICKENING LOOP

By Tina Fakhrid-Deen

*As ISIS imagines a new day, there are low, ambient sounds such as laughter or nature sounds, when applicable. When she speaks of travel, there are images of a floral crown spooling from her scalp with butterflies finding their way to her. There are scorpions nearby, maybe upon her shoulder and at her feet.*

**ISIS:** Out. I want out of this box. If I knew how to change all of this, I would. I wouldn't be so alert, so... reticent. You know? I'd allow myself to slumber and lull. Like a black swan floating on an orange horizon. I'd bring people together for simple meals with clean ingredients and lots of spices like cardamom, smoked paprika, and ginger, lots of ginger. And we'd savor the concert being orchestrated in our mouths, inducing us into more conversation - rich, delicious, honest, and unencumbered. No small talk or minds. We'd all laugh and laugh until we cried, completely undisturbed by our own contentment. We'd drink the finest of wines from small vineyards in South Africa, France and Spain, Chenin Blanc [Shay-non Blonc], Viognier [Vee-Oh-nyay], Tempranillo [Temp-rah-Nee-yoh], drunk on possibilities and good company, only sobered by the profound love in the room. Then we'd take long naps before our journey further into ourselves. I'd travel widely, singing to exotic birds that called out to me and chase bumblebees and migrating Painted Ladies only to catch them gently in my palm. I'd sit them upon the dense jungle of flowers growing from my scalp, so that they can rest and sip and frolic a bit before going back to their lives because we all deserve a break from just surviving. I'd be a beast - wild and brazen. Free. Not a beast of your imagination, but of mine - resplendent, celestial and delicate. No sharp edges or tongues. Round softness. One who could feel or dispense pain if I chose, but why would I bog myself down with the mundanity of strife? Instead, I'd dance and twirl to the melody of the moon with warm tears from the sun streaming down my breasts, bursting into an orgasm of stars. But I can't because we're here. Stuck.

# I AM NOT YOUR TEACHER

By Kayodè Soyemi

**CHARACTERS**
TEACHER: Black.
THE MAN: White. Not visible, but present.

**NOTES ON TEXT**
1. [TEXT] – something TEACHER assists with any form of visual content.
2. [[TEXT]] – something TEACHER assists with photo content.
3. [[[TEXT]]] – something TEACHER assists with drawn, written, or typed content.

**GENERAL NOTES**
TEACHER must be performed by a Black actor, and while it is not gender specific, it is important to understand this comes from the playwright's experience as a Black man.

In the world of this play, TEACHER believes they are one of the last of their kind. While the audience for the performance may be mixed, the audience for the experiment is non-Black.

## I AM NOT YOUR TEACHER

*An introduction song is playing— one of THE MAN's anthems. A "WELCOME!" title is shown. TEACHER appears on screen, dressed nicely, greeting the audience and preparing for this live lecture, ted-talk-like re-education session.*

**TEACHER:** Thank you! Thank you! First, I want to thank The Man for giving me this opportunity and I applaud all of you in the audience for your valiant efforts in seeking to learn. I know several of you have frequented these educational sessions, and you're probably wondering, "How will this end any different?" I can assure you all, that my training will prove necessary for an experiment of this caliber.

A little about me: I was raised in a supermax prison at a location I cannot disclose for possessing less than one gram of... Marijuju. When I was released, I had difficulty acclimating to my newfound freedom. I noticed there was no one out there like me. Of course I ended up getting back into trouble, and sent back to prison. Returning to the system, I needed answers. That's when I discovered I was one of the few Blacks alive. And as of this very session, the only one who can speak about...

*TEACHER reveals the titular visual for the presentation.*

[THE TRUE HISTORY OF THE BLACKS]

There really isn't much out there about us. The current history books don't have much if any information. All I know, as the truth, is what The Man provided for me. I am so grateful. If I... happened to die today, The Blacks will pretty much be extinct. So. I've been commissioned here to share with you the true science, history and politics of how we operated in parts of the world and America... before. I believe it is my duty.

So what is a Black? A Black is a person that lived on this–

*THE MAN signals. A red laser point appears on the body of TEACHER. Fear fills their eyes.*

Or they are otherwise known as a human or homosapien–

*The signal comes again, louder and more aggressive. Another red laser point.*

Or as most of you might know, [[[NIGGER]]]...

*The laser points disappear. TEACHER is relieved.*

That lived on this very planet! Where did they come from? Contrary to popular belief, the history of The Blacks actually predates the [BARACK OSAMA ERA]. Some would argue our history began in the 1990s, with the rise of that hippity-hop and the hit TV show The Family that Matters Enough to Crown a Prince of Bel-Air. But. There were indeed Blacks [BC: BEFORE COLOR]. There is proof that the first Blacks actually came from the African Ocean. The mother-fish known as [OPRAH] to be exact. It wasn't until a massive meteorite full of melanin crashed into what we now know as Wakanda effected the entire continent of Africa, and ultimately, the rest of the world.

The impact from that meteorite changed the course of life on this planet. Radiation from the meteorite spread, melaninating every living organism. For those of you who don't know what melanin is, it is a compound that effects the pigmentation of skin. Everyone has it. There are two forms: [[["PHEO–"]]]melanin is responsible for the white, pinkish, reddish pigmentation found most heavily in people of European descent. And [[["EU–"]]]melanin, the purest and most dangerous form of melanin, also known as "the brown and black compound" was heavily found in ancient Egyptians, Ethiopians, Nigerians, African Americans, and Aboriginal Australians. The evolution of the original Black people–

*THE MAN signals. A red laser point appears.*

Uh, humans– uh Niggers...

*The laser point disappears.*

Marked the beginning of a new era, [AD: AFTER DA-METEOR].

Now, Eumelanin has varying effects on the physical, especially over time. In recent males, the radiation is most commonly represented in the [[ABNORMALLY LARGE PENIS]]. In females, it is noticeable in the wider, child-bearing hips similar to the hips that killed [[KIM KARDASHIAN]]– A hero in The Blacks' community. It also effects physical abilities. While it cancelled the once natural-born, fish-like skills of swimming, we became predominates at hunting for pig skin. Eumelanin gave The Blacks natural defense mechanisms. For instance, the chemical reaction from touching any of The Blacks' hair... It would have made you explode. Or how we became... indistinguishable. This is why I look like all of The Blacks some of you might've seen pictures of.

For 1500 years, Africans made several technological advances. Thinking others all over the world could benefit, 12.5 million of them traveled to the surrounding continents by way of [[MASSIVE FLYING SHIPS [1]]] that could carry up to 600 niggers at a time. More than 10 million landed in the Americas, and [[HARRIET "MOSES" TUBMAN]], a Black with superior navigation skills, made herself 19 trips. The Man calls this [THE MIDDLE PASSAGE]. Once landed, niggers went straight to work, finding that barren southern lands could benefit the most. An agreement of labor was made by the pure will of these immigrated Blacks to turn the south into a place with abundant resources. The following years of the [[CIVIL WORKING RELATIONSHIPS [2]]] helped to make America one of the most productive countries in the world. At no cost, the Black interns joyfully graced the lands with spirituals while they picked and gathered material for tougher clothing-- cotton, quadrupling agriculture production, and introducing a new standard for cooking that emphasized the use of flavor enhancing seasonings.

*THE MAN signals for a break.*

I believe we're just going to take a quick break. Please, I invite you to get some water, take a stretch, whatever you need to do in order to be present with us when we're back. I'll leave you all with some of the content we've gone over to keep your minds and hearts focused on this session.

*TEACHER steps away, leaving something from the presentation on screen.*

*We hear TEACHER, speaking to THE MAN:*

Aye boss, something don't feel right... You hear em? I don't think this stuff really getting through they heads... Maybe... shit... maybe there's some doubt? Maybe they doubting if this actually the truth. Maybe I'm not the one to do this, boss...

*THE MAN signals.*

Hold on, hold on! Listen, listen! You remember you need me! Without me, how you gon' recreate us! I get it you didn't like the "people" slip up but even if I was trying to fuck with your plan it won't change nothing about how they see me! I'm not tryin' to challenge you, I'm just sayin', boss, it don't feel right... Yes. I understand. "This ain't for them. Iss for me..." I'm the only one who can do this... I will comply...

*TEACHER continues to repeat "I will comply" as they return.*

I apologize for that abrupt break, but I am sure glad we took it! Once again, I want to thank The Man. I want to make sure he knows how grateful I am to be here.

*TEACHER takes a moment.*

OK. Where were we? Cotton, Agriculture, Seasonings... These accomplishments made it so the South could not function without the aid and labor of the unpaid Black interns. When many of the interns felt they should migrate North to share their advances, southern representatives challenged the abolitionist movement, because of how it threatened the southern way of life. It violated the agreement, harmed the productivity of the south and ultimately the entire country. Those representatives came together and called themselves [THE CONFEDERACY]. Northern representatives, in retaliation, called themselves [THE UNION]. The arguments between the two sides were so heated, it sparked a war. Niggers were the cause of that war. [THE WAR OF SEPARATION]. 620,000 lives were lost in battle and from disease. The result was an unfortunate Union victory and the 13th Amendment which voided the agreement. Throughout that period of Reconstruction, the tensions from the war continued. State and local laws were passed that would keep "colored" and "white" people, uh... niggers and uh non-niggers segregated. They were nicknamed the [[JIM CROW [3]]] Laws, which condoned violence between the two groups and coined the phrase "separate but equal."

*TEACHER has trouble dealing with this image. Their vision becomes blurry. They are dizzy. They have trouble breathing.*

[SEGREGATION]... Segregation umm... Segregation...was useful in keeping these tensions low, but it didn't last. [MARTIN LUCIFER KING], a radical preacher, sought to end Segregation and create a Black supremacist nation. Under the guise of "civil rights," MLK used various brainwashing powers to take advantage of millions, evident in several organized riots; the most significant being [[THE GREAT RIOT [4]]] on Washington.

The reach of MLK's control put niggers everywhere, and America lit a flame for radical movements all over the world. Governments began creating programs to survey, infiltrate, discredit, and disrupt these acts of certain influence. That worldwide effort to end the spread of this hateful, gang-like mentality targeted dangerous organizations like The Black Panthers and The Nation of Islam, individuals like Malcolm XXX, Ass Hata Shakur, even Fela Coochie and Nelson Mandalorian– specifically for their opposition to police forces and their execution of powers to protect and serve.

Over the next 30 years, The Blacks continued to pollute minds by ways of fashion, sports, music and all forms of entertainment. They took every opportunity to bring their ideas to the mainstream zeitgeist and sway popular opinion. One of the best representations we have of this is Rodney King's vicious attack on four police officers, and the 6 day rioting that followed in which 63 people were killed and over 2,300 injured. "Black sympathy," the brainwashing, is what led [BARACK OSAMA], an illegally cloned result of MLK, to be elected President of the United States.

Osama's election gave niggers the voice they needed to really take control.

They instilled fear and violence in several ways. The riots continued, earning the title the [[BLACK LIVES MATTER MORE [5]]] Movement. It seemed that leading up to and throughout Osama's disaster of a presidency, massive incarceration was the only temporary solvent to limit the full capacity of The Blacks' power. However, a hidden demographic of Americans was able to breakthrough and elect someone with the goal to "Make America Great Again." That goal would lay the foundation for The Man's successful rise.

The Man was able to unify Americans, and later the world, to one mission: get rid of niggers. He calls it "The Black Cleansing." Now, The Man is confident that if I can share with you the truth, he can recreate us the proper way...

Unfortunately, he is wrong.

*THE MAN signals. A laserpoint appears.*

Whatever justification The Man has for getting rid of Black people don't matter! He got America– THE WORLD to believe that we a threat. Whether it's the culture, or penis size, it's not going to change your opinion of me!

*Another signal, then another, louder and aggressive. Several laserpoints appear, all targeting various parts of TEACHER.*

You don't care bout my feelings. You never will! Because no amount of teaching science or history or politics is gon convince you that I'm human! The Black Cleansing!? Call it what it is, THE BLACK MASSACRE!!!!!! (to THE MAN) As I'm standing here, right now, the last nigga on this planet, tell me that I am not human!! I WILL NOT COMPLY! I AM NOT YOUR TEACH—

*We are left with an empty screen, no presentation, no TEACHER. Maybe they've died, or maybe they've beat THE MAN.*

1. [[MASSIVE FLYING SHIPS]][a]

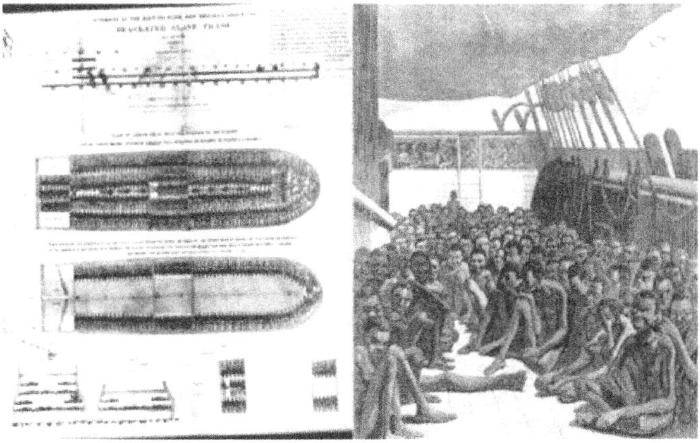

2. [[CIVIL WORKING RELATIONSHIPS]][b]

3. [[JIM CROW LAWS][c]

4. [[THE GREAT RIOT]][d]

5. [[BLACK LIVES MATTER MORE]][e]

---

[a] Hulton Archive/Getty Images
[b] Lightfoot/Getty Images
[c] Chicago Historical Society
[d] National Archives
[e] 2016 Pacific Press

# WALK A MILE IN MY RAGE

By Gary Earl Ross

Rage can be terrifying but I want you to UNDERSTAND.

Imagine you are six and overhear that your grandmother's first husband, your biological grandfather, was murdered by white men in South Carolina in 1925.

Imagine at twelve taking your five-year-old brother back to the push merry-go-round at a public park because white kids won't let him ride. A blonde girl of five says, "Brown people are the worst people in the world. Even God don't like 'em."

Imagine at fourteen walking along the railroad tracks parallel to Ferry with your friend Drake and having two police officers stop you, guns drawn, to ask what you're doing. "Talking about the future," you say. True, because you are both honor students who dare to dream.

Once when you inadvertently cut off another car, the driver, a woman, screams, "Nigger!" You would prefer being called an idiot or an asshole—some insult that keeps your humanity intact instead of calling hers into question.

A black man in a doorway catches 41 bullets while trying to comply with a police request for ID by taking out his wallet. A child with a toy gun is shot dead without even being ordered to drop the weapon. You see black people shot in the back, shot in their yards, shot outside stores, shot in their homes, shot while jogging, even shot while sleeping, You see them choked to death or knelt upon until they choke to death. You see far too many killers walk free.

And you want to scream.

So your anger becomes rage. But even in rage you know that you and others like you *still believe in the American Dream.* The day you all stop—the day all the marginalized believe there is no place in the country for darker skin and other differences, that bigotry is beyond redemption—is the day America burns to the ground.

# HashtagTheBlackGirl

By Cashel Campbell

This pain isn't new.
I don't matter.
My voice doesn't matter.
My love is ignorable.
My existence is a dream.
I would have come and gone and no one would have seen me,
or heard me.

My hair
is good enough to be touched, poked & pulled.
It's good enough to be a wig, costume or extension.
Nappy, Napturia, coiled hair #0A at the beauty supply—
you won't buy it.
I can be looked at & ogled at & asked out loud
in public
at work
or at play
if my OWN grown hair "is real"?

I'm living in the biggest invisible cage.

I am a freak show,
Sandra Bartmann 2016, big ass in tow. And the ass,
my ass, the big asses
the big brown asses
can be packaged in
shorts & jeans
& injected in Central America
or in North
if you want.

The Black asses matter
& they can be fashioned
& touched & fucked & wanted &

"she's really only hot because of that big ole ass".

Big fat Black ass, my own men's glory—

(but just my ass
change my skin and hair texture— toooooooooo Black).

Brown skin,
turns brown gold in summer, I love her.
It's a stain, identifier.
More pokes, more rubs, more stares,
"why is your skin so shiny"?
Tanning salons, franchise richness that's selling Brown girl on a bed.
White or Hispanic women twins in summer cause
"they get Blacker than me", apparently...

but then summer fades
& they're back to the privilege package, the one that doesn't include the tan.
The tan that reminds me every day
that my beauty and body parts are wanted,
just not me, not the person inside.

Lips for sale too.
Selling these might mean not hearing from a Black Woman...
can't speak how I feel
can't wear my own hair
can't be strong cause then I'm scary
can't cry cause then I'm showing weakness & shaming the Ancestors
Can't confide in my Brothers cause far as they're concerned it's all in our heads,
these complex complexes.
Can't stick up for my feelings or my people cause some other group needs their needs to be met from the ones that look like me—

Wet nurse wasn't enough?
Slave bed warmer wasn't enough? Nanny to ALL the babies isn't enough?

Give it to the Black girl!

She can fix
and be
and do anything and she's available and naked.

And that's how I feel,
Naked
Unsupported
Invisible.

And I
I really really, REALLY don't matter.

-HashtagTheBlackGirl

# to kneel or not to kneel

By Bryan-Keyth Wilson

*The national anthem begins to play and men dressed in football uniforms enter. As the music begins to play one of them steps out from the group and begins to speak.*

**man in red:**
to kneel/or not to kneel / that is the question

whether 'tis nobler in the mind to endure

the social injustices and prejudices of this great country

or to use my freedoms allotted to me by our founding fathers

who were the writers of the 1st Amendment. to kneel/ to stand

no/ nd by kneel to say we end the systematic racism

nd the assassination of black men in the streets

'tis a consummation devoutly to be wished/ to kneel/ to stand

to stand/ perchance the opportunity to stand for a cause

ay/ there's the rub

for in standing it is an act of valor and patriotism

but truthfully standing for this cause brings bout a bowed head

five fingers clinched in a fist with an arm extending to the heavens

bending at the knee as you do for your god/your bride to be

tis not an act of submission

tis an act of honor and veracity

within this axiom/ one is forced to see one's self

looking upon a country whose land is free nd brave

denounces every principle and founding law

the proletariats obtuse gaze is fueled by a president
whose closeted racist ideals begin to show
americas anthem reads/

their blood has washed out their foul footsteps pollution
no refuge could save the hireling and slave
from the terror of flight or the gloom of the grave
and the star/spangled banner in triumph doth wave
o'er the land of the free and the home of the brave

what say you to this folly of speech
soft you now/ i pray these words may heal
but for when this song is played
i will continue to kneel

# WHY I WAS LATE TODAY, AND WILL PROBABLY ALWAYS BE LATE AS A BLACK WOMAN

By Liz Morgan

My father begged me to never take the bus
And like 1950 something
All the negroes are sitting at the back of this one
Coincidence, I am sure
But one of us negroes is drunk and loud and vulgar
He boasts about his time in jail
And this negro throws the other N word around like a Jim Crow boomerang
And I feel my skin get hot
All that melanin
Absorbing the sun but
Still reflecting off each other
It's blinding such that we become indistinguishable to others
And I fear that the beige ears and blue eyes in front of me are thinking we are all drunk and loud and vulgar
My brown eyes catch the brown eyes of the sister next to me as we confide in each other
Our silent shame
We know they hate him
I think they hate us
I start to hate myself
And I too hate him for making me hate myself again
I think
And suddenly
Like he could hear my thoughts
this stranger decides to direct his drunk, loud, vulgar self at me

I politely decline his conversation
Several times
The way all women have rehearsed the structured improvisation of harassment
That always ends in insults and FUs
He says I am a stereotypical black woman
I wonder about stereotypical kettles and pots
And just as his harsh words escalate, the world stops
Or just the bus
(I'm still not sure)
As the driver comes back to find out what the problem is
And this drunk and loud and vulgar man who has been annoying everyone
But only really bothering me
Stands up
Grabs his only weapon:
his clothed black cock
To defend his right to talk to me
Who has declined this conversation
The driver walks away
Back to the front of the bus
And finally his drunk and loud and vulgar brain figures it out:
His place on the food chain
This white woman is pulling the Trump card
She is restoring Law and Order
And as we wait for the police
On the side of the highway
This drunk and loud and vulgar man
Quiets down and sobers up
To apologize and beg this stereotypical black woman for mercy
He asks me to tell them we don't have a problem

He calls me babe
I make him say my name
He tells me his life will be messed up if he doesn't get to where he's going
I know that I will be messed up if he ends up in cuffs
Or in a coffin
Because of this night
This night that reminds me of how much I hate being black and a woman
This curse
I give him my phone to call his family
I remind him to pray
I comfort this man who has cursed me and everyone who looks like me
And when three cop cars show up
I walk through the aisle of blue eyes
As they burn through my melanin
skin peeling off to reveal a layer of redboned privilege
My summer tan disappears and I code switch
Into the type of girl who feels safe around boys in blue
And I try really really hard to make this black life matter before they make the kind of judgement that cannot be undone
And after they put him in the back of one of three cop cars that showed up in response to one drunk, loud, vulgar man
Of color
One of the boys in blue asks me again if I knew this man
I tell them again that I don't but perhaps at this point I do
I feel like Peter denying the Son of God before his crucifixion
The cop looks at me in disbelief and says "then why did you get off the bus with him?"
And I want to say because Trayvon,
because Mike,

because Eric,

because Philando,

because Alton

because... He is drunk and loved and vulnerable and his life matters

And I forgive him

But this character I am playing doesn't talk like that

So I upwardly inflect "I just wanted you to have all the information"

And I leave the boys in blue to join the blue eyes on the bus

We take off and I pretend that we are headed to the same destination

And maybe we are but somehow I always find myself lost

Delayed at these invisible intersections

# HOW DARE YOUR?!

By Jonathon Benjamin

How dare you... Why must I start a conversation with my being black? Why is it always a matter of race, with me? Why can't we just be people and not Black or White? (a beat) You. Tell. Me. Because I remember the same history lesson from every year of twelve years of school that explained how an entire race of people were taken—no, stolen—from their homeland and brought to this (looking around) New World. I remember the arguments that the slaves were sold by their own people, but (shaking head) no, no, no. There were strings and puppets and figures moving behind the scenes. It came down to money for the man in power... the men still in power, today. (pause) You ask why? You have the audacity to ask me, why? I'll tell you that for 246 years of forced, brutish and inhuman American Slavery, a people had their names taken, their families separated and watched countless lives lost on the stench-soaked Middle Passage. That whip-fashioned generation of Black America crawled up from the muck of the plantation and stood, albeit unsteadily, with a bowed back under the calculated eyes of these United States. Why must I always state that I am African American? (pause) So that you know, even if for just one moment, that I understand. Oh, yes, I understand it with my mind, body and spirit that I am only here because of the hard work and broken dreams of the four million slaves that came before me. My soul cries out at this ignorance I must answer, today. (pause) It is a matter of Black and White because that is what America has made of it, what it was built on. It's the way we live. This is why I cannot walk into a department store without catching the watchful eye of a guard, while you sit to enjoy a day at the yacht club with your friends... You ask me all these things as if you're the one who should be offended. I know my history—GO READ A BOOK!

# LOST GENERATION

By SIRI MANI

I need you to care. Not about yourself or obtaining your wealth.
I need you....to look around.
Sirens are becoming a familiar sound
Our faces are getting used to being put in the ground And for what?
Well see I have this theory. It goes like,
"My mind is powerful and that's why they fear me."
Cuz if I don't see probable cause i might not go down willingly
And some of y'all might think that's the kid in me But for you not to be angry Are you kidding me?
My generation isn't lost.
We're angry.
And instead of ignoring the problem to focus on ourselves we turn our attention in an attempt to help and
At times we do it wrong.
But to me, anything is better than just playing along
Now if this generation is lost.
It's cuz they're out here killing the ones meant to lead us.
The ones with the strong mental thesis who see us for more than what we appear to be.
Yeah, they see the drive, but also the fear me.
This generation isn't lost.
We're scared.
To death.
Like a wounded animal only hostile to protect whatever we have left .
So yeah we lash.
Oh yeah we spazz.
We black out It happens so fast.
And... In an attempt to express ourselves I guess we forget the beauty in everything that we have...
So we destroy it.
But then again, years ago my American history teacher told me there is always anarchy before order so...

Is this that transition or just hopeful wishing?
Am i out here talking to walls right now or are you actually listening?
See this isn't the future we envisioned and maybe that's why we're mad.
Now I won't take shots at mom's and dad's
But why'd you tell us there were infinite opportunities for us
When two or three seemed to be all we really had?
Here I am thinking the worst adulthood would give me is a terrible boss...
Why wasn't i warned about the friends I've lost?
But we're the lost generation...
Na, we just grew up quick
So excuse us for lacking imagination
But we want compensation for the lies we bought.
Just carry the thought—
Most of us are still waiting to grow up and be astronauts
Now ask me what I wanted to be in the 5th grade,
I'd say a police officer... So I can save lives.
And I guess that's just a funny example of how time flies once you've opened your eyes.
It was never my intention to despise "the good guys."
Which leads me to a series of unfortunate questions with equally unfortunate answers
Mr. Officer (on megaphone)
I wonder... If you saw grandma's face at the family reunion
When she counts 7 instead of 8 grandsons.. Then would you show remorse for taking the life of that one?
Or if whenever you shot someone you heard the scream from their mother instead of the bullet leaving the chamber.. Now would you understand our anger?
See i have so many questions but i fear if i ask I'll be answered by Smith & Wesson.
Even if the point was simply to teach an officer a lesson
If I'm killed over this simple disagreement...
I think we all know who the judicial systems protecting..
Cuz in a world where a 7 year old can be killed in her sleep and

it's considered justified.
Are you really surprised at how many of us have died?
See we're a generation losing hope, but we're not hopeless
Some of us are out here trying to fight for what we believe in and no one seems to notice Instead of having our back they go behind it and scold us.
Instead of telling us what to do, Why not stand up and show us?

# INERTIA

By James J. Johnson

*KEVIN GIBSON, African-American man in his 20s, is seated with a cellphone in his hand, that he mindlessly toys with throughout his speech. If speech is filmed, maybe we don't see the phone until the final moment. He is dressed relatively well, casual or business casual. He is educated but grew up in a working class community, so he is a professional switcher of codes.*

**KEVIN:** Newton's first law, inertia, is defined as "the property of matter by which it retains its state of rest or its velocity along a straight line so long as it is not acted upon by an external force." Shout out to Dictionary.com!

Urban Dictionary goes on to say, "Don't confuse this with momentum," which is "the impetus gained by a moving object."

It's like Urban Dictionary gets me, as a black man, and my aversion for being confused for someone or something I am not.

*Beat.*

So tonight, I am leaving my job at the NIH! Bethesda, Murrland, muhfuggah! I am a scientist, a physicist. I may be a scrub physicist -- I did just start there last year, nahmean -- but I know my way around Stefan's Law, Newton's Laws, Law of Conservation of Energy -- I know some laws. Plus I got receipts! From Johns Hopkins AND M.I.T.!

So I am leaving my job, right? In my car. I am in motion. I'm a little tired, but nothing out-of-the-ordinary. I'm cruising, top-down. . . in my head, I'm cruising top-down in a convertible, but in reality I'm in a damn Kia. A scrub car for a scrub physicist rolling down scrubby-ass Wisconsin Avenue late at night.

I am leaving my job. I just want to get home. I am retaining my velocity. I'm bobbing my head to J. Cole. I am in motion. Inertia. My heartbeat's steady, thumping. J. Cole is thumping. Then in my rearview, BOOM. Blue, red lights, flashing. Steady heartbeat now racing. Breath stopping. J. Cole still thumping. Foot braking. I pull over along the side of Wisconsin and an officer angles his car to the rear of mine. Though initially startled by the sudden burst of lights and sounds, I remind myself that I am a moderately charming man.

Chin up, Bro. You got this.

But the cop gets out of his car, slams his door and is up on my driver's side door with the momentum of a bullet.

*Beat.*

He is barking at me and it takes a minute for me to orient my brain, to understand what he's saying. "I need you out of the car!" he shouts.

"Hold up, what?! What did I -- ? You need my license and -- ?" Before I can finish my sentence, he's opening my car door and pulling me from my car. Now I understand a lot of laws of physics. "To every action there is an equal and opposite reaction." Newton's third law. I do not understand the law that this cop is operating under currently. My instinct to survive overrules my reason, and I can feel my body in a struggle with this stranger. I don't want to be in a struggle with this man, but we are now tussling.

"Kevin Gibson!" He starts. "You're wanted for strong-arm robbery. Stop resisting. Stop resisting. Stop. Resisting. Stop." I'm trying to tell him that he's got the wrong Kevin Gibson, and that I was just trying to get home from work, but our bodies have already built up this momentum. I can see him reaching down at his belt, and I'm trying to get out of his grasp. I am finally able to get the bottom of my foot onto the car and push off. We both go down. He breaks his grasp, and I jump up and start running. I'm hauling ass down Wisconsin. All I can hear is his fading voice behind me shouting, "Stop! Stop! Stop!"

And then a gunshot.

*Beat.*

He missed me. Because I'm still running. I didn't feel a thing. I'm back in motion. It's like the world around me hushed so that all I could hear was the pounding of my feet and the thumping of my chest. For the first time I noticed how chilly it was for a June night. It's crazy. I can see my breath.

As I neared home, ten miles later, I slowed down because I fully expected to see cop cars swarming my spot, or at least the neighborhood.

But nothing. The burbs were even quieter than normal. Crickets.

*Beat.*

So now here I am, waiting. Not sure how long I got before the cops show up. I have been home for about a half-hour. They obviously got the wrong Kevin Gibson. Maybe I can explain to them . . . Shit. I can't be on the run. I'm not that kinda dude. But I fought a fucking cop and ran. And not just ran, but outran a damn bullet! I could be a black hero.

*KEVIN notices the phone in his hand for the first time.*

Maybe I can find out something about the other Kevin.

*Long pause as he is intently focused on his phone. After some time passes:*

(reading to himself) "Friends mark the one-year anniversary of the shooting death of young NIH physicist at the hands of local officer?"

*Beat.*

"Case of mistaken identity?"

*Beat.*

"Can't believe it's been a year, Kevin. . . Still miss you like it was yesterday?" "I wish I could hear your laugh one more time, nerd."

Ah, Cyndi. You're the nerd.

What the fuck?

I'm dead?

*Beat.*

I've been dead for a year?

Whoa. I'm a ghost.

A black-ass ghost.

"Energy can neither be created nor destroyed but it can be transformed from one form to another."

*Pause, as he considers it all. All of it. Then. . .*

If I'm a ghost, then how I got phone service?

# RED CARD

By Michael Rishawn

*The locker room. COURTNEY packs his bag. Wilson stands before him.*

**COURTNEY:** Wilson, I've always been a handful of minorities in elite schools. I've learned to tone down my size, my blackness, by becoming shy, introverted, friendly—careful not to scare the rich little white kids or their parents. Their ignorance took away my self-confidence and my sanity, I mean, I've been told I'm not black enough it's nearly destroyed me. But see, the not fitting in part, makes you think your talent on the pitch'll make up for it. So, you overcompensate. Create a persona separate from who you really are just to use it as motivation to gain respect from playing a game. Make a fool of yourself at times. Anything in the quest to one day feel 'cool.' Anyone else in my shitty locker room situation wouldn't take everything so personally, right? Say, 'fuck it you're making millions, you're living your dream!' I mean, I'm a rookie who's averaged better than some of the old heads on this team. Most of them won't ever touch the numbers I put up! So, yea, I took what I wanted from the people who refused to give it to me—I demanded it! That white washed, hermetically sealed bubble I was educated in, didn't provide those lessons... And yea, what I did was wrong, I know that, but the worst of it? Being called a snitch by my own teammates. I won't go down for it. Hell no. And if that's it for me, then so be it, if that means I gotta lace up my cleats and lock'em away, ok. Cuz honestly this shit don't matter. None of it does. The fans, the federation, the team... Nothing matters besides my family, a few close friends, and my own happiness... But even that doesn't fucking matter because I'll still be looked at as the faggot kid who couldn't handle the locker room.

*Courtney slams the locker door, throws his cleats in the bin and exits.*

# OUTER INNER MONOLOGUE

By Louis DeVaughn Nelson

*Andre Johnson. A classically trained Black actor.*

*A Rehearsal Studio in New York City. Late Autumn. Afternoon, 2019.*

*ANDRE, a spritely yet composed professional actor enters. He addresses the casting directors.*

**ANDRE:** Good Day. I'm Andre Johnson, auditioning for the role of Robert. For my comedic monologue I'm doing Bobby from A Chorus Line, and I'll be singing "My Girlfriend Who Lives in Canada" from Avenue Q.

*He begins a series of quick warmup exercises. Crosses stage left, finds his position, steps forward, and begins.*

"No no – moving right along.

Let's see...

Do you wanna know about all the wonderful and exciting things that have happened to me in my life – or do you want to know The Truth?"

*He hesitates. He goes blank. A bit of shock, not entirely off-putting. He begins again.*

Uh...

"No. No...

...moving right along" I – um, um...

Fuck!

Wait.

Sorry.

I – may I start again?

(beat)

Right – breathe.

*He does another breathing exercise and then pours on the charm.*

Alright, here we go. I'm just going to restart this, control alt delete it for you. Take it from one.

*He crosses stage right and then back to center and performs the signature step forward again.*

"No no, moving right along. Let's see. Let's, see. Let's –

Do you wanna know about all the – all the..."

Sorry, shit. I can't believe I'm totally blanking.

(beat)

I know, I know, but I'm so not that guy.

I mean, I've done this show thrice and this monologue is indelibly etched into my psyche and I can't even –

*ANDRE is interrupted.*

Oh sorry. I know. Time. Time is money. Here we go.

"Do you want to – do you wanna know about all the wonderful and exciting...things or do you wanna know the truth?"

*ANDRE stammers again.*

Uh. Uh.

This has never happened. Is it ok if I do the song first? I don't need accompaniment.

(beat)

Yes, yes, definitely – thank you. So sorry.

*He takes another moment. After deciding a change of place might help, he warms up his voice a bit and then begins.*

(singing)

"Oh – oh I

wish you could meet my girlfriend,

my girlfriend who lives in..."

(beat)

I – yeah. This isn't working. I was going to. I mean, I am. But I just. I can't. Or, I don't want to.

I – I shouldn't be doing this, and I'm sorry I don't want to waste your time but...

My monologue, my song that I chose, I tried to get as close to something that was me but wasn't. But is. They say you should never lose yourself entirely in a character but that's why I became an actor. Isn't that the best part?

When I saw the call for this I went against my "better judgment" (no offense to your production) I LOVE YOUR WORK which is the real reason why I'm here, but is there a place for me where I want to be no matter who I am or in this instance who I'm becoming?

I'd have a whole lot of nothing if I refused to succumb to typecasting but there's only so many of those roles I can take before I – I mean, the thought of playing Homeless Man #2 or Drug Dealer, or Doorman, or a Civil Rights Leader, or Driver or Wife Beater or Featured Dancer... well you know.

Don't get me wrong – I'm grateful to be a working actor – hashtag blessed – but if I'm in the blackground One. More. Time.

That wasn't a threat or anything, I can't even kill a roach in my apartment that I share with three people half of which is a couple and her boyfriend is so damn lazy, this one time – that's besides the point.

When I was in college – freshman year – I auditioned for the Fall Main Stage Production of You Can't Take it With You. I wanted, no, needed the role of Donald – you know the handyman who was hooking up with the maid a la Porgy and Bess? The role originally written for an "African-American"?

Well, I got a standing O at the audition – I wore overalls and everything. I walked like Donald, I talked like Donald, I was Donald, and everybody knew it.

(beat)

A week later and no dice.

I went to the show – and...

I went to the show and they cast a Russian guy, a junior, very handsome might I add. The part of Rheba, his opposite, was played by this Latina – she was a junior I think. Anyway, they smothered her in so much white powder you could see a cloud of smoke coming from her the entire time like that character from Snoopy, the one who was always dirty. It wasn't the Black one, was it? Ugh, never mind.

It was probably the best lesson I ever got. I can't complain too much, at least it wasn't black face.

But I'm here today hoping that I can be more to you than Raisin in the Sun or Othello or To Kill a Mockingbird or what else is there? Well, you know.

*ANDRE steps back.*

And scene.

*He starts to exit and then returns.*

And I'm gay.

And you know, Well – I don't know which one to exploit. The gay part or the black part. Put them together and it's a MESS.

That's why I chose A Chorus Line (which as aforementioned I've been in several times) and that's why I chose the "gay" character from Avenue Q.

The first time I was in A Chorus Line I played Tony because I was the only one at this small community theater who could tap dance – of course I had to Black it up the best I could even though he was Italian but you know what they say about eye talians or at least that was our little joke backstage.

The second time I played Greg but instead of being Jewish they made me Muslim despite the fact that Black Jews actually exist.

The last time I played shit Ricky and I was all

(singing)

“Gimme the ball gimme the ball gimme the ball yeah!”

And I just...I can’t.

If you don’t cast me – or if you do, as an experiment or whatever, which I know you won’t, just consider this one little tidbit. We’re all actors and so much of what we do is presenting a vision that sometimes relies on momentary suspension of disbelief and I know sometimes the right look is the right look. Even when you’re making something new those rules of traditional standards and inherent habits can be hard to break.

But all I ever wanted to do is be Harold Hill.

*ANDRE hesitates and exits.*

# A GATHERING OF OLD MEN

By Gladys W. Muturi

*MAT, 60s, African American, entered with a shotgun and gave a determined look at his wife.*

**MAT:** What's the matter with me? What's the matter with me? All these years we've been living together, woman, and you ask me, "What's the matter with me?" The years we done struggled in George Medlow's field, making him richer and richer, and us poorer and poorer and you still don't know what's the matter with me? The years I done stood in that backyard and cussed at God, the years I done stood out on that front Garry and cussed the world, the times I done come home drunk and beat you for no reason at all-and woman, you still don't know what's the matter with me? Oliver, woman! Oliver. May God rest his soul. How they let him die in the hospital because he was black. No doctor to serve him, let him bleed to death, cause he was black. And you ask me what's the matter with me?

He works in mysterious ways. Give an old nigger like me one more chance to do something with his life. He gives me that chance, and I'm taking it. I know I'm old and I may be crazy but I'm staying here fighting.

# IT'S OVER, QUEEN MYA

By Sharece M. Sellem

*MAX records a breakup video for his now ex-girlfriend Mya. Taking a deep breath, he presses record.*

**MAX:** We have to stop. THIS has to stop. I can't even get a word in with you and today, I've had enough. I can't take it anymore. I am mentally, physically, and spiritually drained. Lie after lie, exaggeration after every damn exaggeration, I just can't. I can't. So, it's over. And I mean it...THIS time. For real. It's not gonna be us going back and forth. It's not gonna be you showing up to my place... tryna lure me back in with that lotion you wear that I like and general tso's from Asia Wok. I'm officially done. Matter fact, I still have your Living Single DVD season collection over here and I will send it to you in the mail. No need for you to come over. I'm gonna tell you something and I know this is going to hurt and I know things will never be the same... we will probably never talk again. And that's ok. That's what I want. A Clean break. After this video there's no reason to call or come over. Those days are over.

> *Takes a deep breath and is already regretting what he's getting ready to say.*

I am seeing Misha (beat). You were right (beat). The times you saw the text messages we were just cool but it's something more now. Look, I didn't want things to go this way, but it did and honestly, I can't really apologize because, truthfully, you were trippin! For the life of me I cannot take one more drag down argument with you calling me out my name, bringing my family into it, going to my friends, going to my job... I just can't. I'm in a different space now. Misha gets me. She doesn't go off and she doesn't disrespect me. She holds me down. She actually listens to me when I talk about Irish sea moss and Dr. Sebi recipes. She cares about me, for me. She's chill. And she's into art. She understands my art. This is something you never took the time to understand. You just cared about what I could do for you. This is just not me... not anymore.

You see this painting? You probably don't remember because you never took the time to really listen to me.

I painted this as a representation of our people. And you couldn't understand. You know what she said? She said she felt like the ancestors were guiding my paintbrush to create my own story. And that's when it hit me that I need to clean out evil. I need to do right... by ME. I've spent all this time chasing after you when you would have your episodes and wasted so much time on bull. I'm ready for a new me. A new chapter. A new life. A wife.

*A shift in thought, feeling bad for Mya.*

I'm sorry, Mya, but this is goodbye. I want to wish you well and I really hope you fix the broken little girl inside of you who needs healing. We all need healing. As a people we need healing. Listen to your ancestors. Look at yourself. Look at your world. Why don't you paint a new story. I'm sorry it had to be this way, but it's only for the best. (softening) Look, you're beautiful, no doubt... you're a Queen. We just need to elevate and stop tearing each other down. I hope, in your next relationship, that you choose a King you will respect and honor.

*MAX can't believe he's saying this.*

You deserve it. 'Aight. Well... it's time for me to go. If I see you around town I'll say hi, it's not like I won't speak. Just know that I'm elevating. And I hope you do too. Much love, Queen Mya. Peace.

# UNBECOMING TRAGEDY

A Ritual Journey Toward Destiny

By T. R. Riggins

*A solitary prison cell. A Dream and Memory: A faint percussion of DRUMS which rises to accompany the progression of scene. TERRENCE, a Black Man, perhaps in silhouette, enters light as if seeking refuge...*

**TERRENCE:** My kingdom, my kingdom! Its rooms once teeming with the riches of talent, magic, beauty, and love now void of all save enveloping madness. Its pillars and posts of promise collapsed and crumbled about me. And its windows once looking out over a realm of flowing and fertile wonder, now grimed and shattered opaque shards of fracture and doom. Woven wool carpets upon which once I danced now tattered disheveled string and twine entangling to hang me! I am bound and gagged, subdued by the insidious urge propelling me toward the precipice of my fatality. I stumble upon a sacred circle drawn of black bodies on the sandy cusp of the Pacific horizon. The drums have commenced.

I am moved yet unmoving as the drums' percussion resounds against the tide of my desire and pulses through me but I can not command my body to dance within the sacred circle into the realm of salvation. I stand betwixt ebb and flow witnessing others bend and reach, whirling about, unbound. I alone am bound. Liberation summons me. Sacred gems risen from the ocean, visiting ashore, mercy in my midst and reach, urging me to witness the majesty of their sacrifice appealing to my strength to stand, to stand through the beating of the drums and dance that I may move purged and pure toward discovering my song and fulfilling my promise and purpose before the ritual of untimely death claims my body. Why can't I offer myself up to the beating beauty, offer my body to flex and bend, lunge and thrust, lift and swoop, turn and whirl, reach and fold away, out of the possession of this too familiar fiend and toward the embrace of my Nila, my daughter, my mother and father, brother and sister, my lover, my kindreds, my self.

I can not find release from the binding urge teeming to subvert my future, it is the only salve I yearn to nurse these festering wounds sustained doing battle in this epic war, this life, never ending, never won. A drawn out theatre of hostilities, tedium ad nauseam infinitum. Is there anyone else battle weary and war torn? Mama, Daddy!?! Daddy, Mama!? My kingdom, my kingdom! The urge becomes my craze, the force of which reigns over my will to stand and dance against it. Even with the foreknowledge of my self betrayal and doom it becomes a seeming reasonable thought in the language of my mind campaigning against the sanity and sanctity of self love. My craze, diminishing all arguments against itself, now becomes my vision and prophecy from which there is no escape. The drums are beating yet I am being played upon. My kingdom, my kingdom... My kingdom for a crack pipe!?!!

*The Drums cease.*

BLACKOUT

LIGHTS UP

*TERRENCE wakes up abruptly out of dream/memory, standing or sitting in the middle of cell.*

My kingdom for a crack pipe!?!!

*Looks about realizing then proclaims and/ or confesses...epiphanous, as if introducing himself.*

I AM A TRAGEDY!

*Silence. Weighing the gravity.*

But once... once I was a boy. Or was I? Maybe I was actually born a tragedy and somehow grew into a boy or not ever really a boy at all but a fledgling tragedy. (has idea)

I'd really prefer being somewhere in the middle. Somewhere betwixt a comedy and a tragedy. Between a damn shame and a goddamn pity.

*He thinks, then takes off his shirt and does a few burpees before...*

*GUNSHOT. He falls as if shot.*

*Quickly standing.*

I was born on February 22, 1965 within twenty four hours of the assassination of Malcolm X. I was delivered while the echoing report of the shotgun blasts still permeated the atmosphere. And of the birth matter which covered my nakedness I'm certain a few splotches of blood were Malcolm's. I was born in the wake of tragedy.

*Sound of gunshot drop then stand.*

On April 4, 1968 Martin Luther King Jr. was assassinated while standing on the balcony of the Lorraine Motel. He was pronounced dead at 7:05 p.m. The next morning at nursery school during a moment of reflection for Dr. King I stood up in the midst of the circle gathering in a state of profound grief and exclaimed "There is no promised land!" An event documented by the school administrator. And a letter was sent to my mother. At three I stood disillusioned and in the shadow of tragedy.

*Begin to African Boot Dance.*

In 1973, when I was eight, my mother decided that my brother, sister and my refuge from tragedy might be found in the Black Nationalist Movement so she enrolled us in The New Age Afrikan School at the corner of Western Ave and Vernon Blvd and we were given Afrikan names. I became...Nkosi.

*Recites Red Black and Green flag salute in Swahili and English alternately.*

Sisi ni weusi tuna nguvu tume azimia. Tume kuja shuleni kushuhudia ukweli wa giza na nguvu. We are black we are strong we are determined. We have come to school to bear witness to blackness truth and strength. Nyekundu nyekundu ni kwa damu ambayo haijapotea bila kutumika. Nyeusi. Nyeusi ni kwa kofia ya familia ya watu wote wa Kiafrika ulimwenguni. Kijani. Kijani kibichi ni kwa ajili ya kilimo cha maisha mapya. Red red is for the blood that has not been lost uselessly. Black black is for the family hood of all Afrikan people around the world." "Green green is for the cultivation of new life. I am a black and proud warrior dedicated to the liberation of my people. My purpose is to protect the black community and its people from all oppressors and to bring about a mental awareness of black feelings, freedom, and effort. Halala.

*Gunshot and drop then stands.*

One summer evening in 1974, Jomo our leader who I only remember as the powerful tall man with the enormous afro and the fierce look of troubled but determined wisdom was murdered. Shotguns and machetes blasted and butchered him and his wife, Chakulia, who was brimming with child. Our community fractured with devastation and grief. At nine years old I learned that there is no refuge from tragedy — even where we cultivated Blackness and celebrated Afrika. So at the age of nine without the protection and discipline of a father, a community or God, more about that later, and right under the gaze of my momma, my beautiful overburdened momma, I, retrospectively speaking, set upon my inevitable journey toward becoming tragedy. (to wall but looking beyond) Now here I am. And being such there is nowhere for me except prison. Or Death. (a revelation) Or... or else... the Theatre where tragedy is highly regarded.

*Covers his face with his hand then removes it, smiling broadly he places it in front of his face again then removes it frowning broadly. He repeats respective to the word pairings.*

Happy, sad...smile, frown...laugh, cry...Light, dark...white, black...comedy, tragedy...happy, smile, laugh, light, white, comedy...sad, frown, cry, dark, black, tragedy.

*TERRENCE raises both hands as if being confronted by a police officer who has a gun drawn.*

BLACKOUT

# WHEN IT RAINS

By J. J. Tingling

Our ancestors are in the rain.

With each drop they cover us
in their love,
blessings,
forgiveness,
hope,
and redemption.

To cleanse.
To nourish.

Hydration to the core.
To renew and replenish.

They remind us we are not weak, we are worn.

To fight another day we must heal and reevaluate.

The moment we decide to continue,
we have no longer failed but merely stumbled.

Prepare.

There is growth after rain.

Drink your honey, ginger, lemon, apple cider vinegar tea and prepare.

Growth is Coming.

# THE SLEEPING COP

By Max King Cap

As the candidate firefighter I always sat third watch. The solitude was enjoyable, I passed most nights unmolested. On one of these nights I met the old, weary cop with thinning blonde hair turning white; he was dangerously overweight. Beat cops are there to show you they are regular folks. Like those officers who warn schoolkids about drugs. The weary cop was not one of those. His wheezing would scare them, his obese waddle would incite giggles. And there was the frightening chance he might drop dead in a classroom full of children. That very thought occurred to me the first time I saw him. As he came nearer I raised my hand in a fraternal wave but he did not respond, his oversized arm perhaps too burdensome to lift, or simply quizzical to see a Black man as a crew member at a previously all White firehouse.

"I'm just going to sit a little while in the back, if that's alright." He looked as if he were going to collapse. "I'll just rest a few minutes then I'll be out of your hair."

I watched him sway side-to-side, like a sailor in rough water, toward our salon of mismatched furniture, where the TV showed sports all day. I wasn't sure my fat copper would survive the night. And if he died it would follow the rest of my career.

"Did you hear about the candidate who let a cop die in the firehouse? No first aid, no alarm, no nothing."

What sadistic lieutenant had sentenced my unfit copper to foot patrol? Walking his nighttime beat he would first feel a tightness in his chest and a tingling in his arm. The doctor's brochure? In his locker. Then squeezing pressure spreading to his neck and jaw, a sudden dizziness overcomes and he is face down on the pavement, one eye staring at blackened chewing gum cemented to the sidewalk. He has had that harsh waking dream many times. I checked on him, he was already asleep on the ratty recliner, heavily snoring. Watching him expand and contract I imagined his younger, slimmer self newly badged on the department, a disperser of harmlessly gathered boys. I was one of those boys. We deserved scrutiny, our skin invited it.

Jackson Park is lengthy public garden, stretching from the University of Chicago down to the Highlands, my neighborhood, a lower middleclass colored section of the city. At its bottom sprawls a public golf course where duffers slice and hook their drives to bushy fence-line. Collecting these wayward balls was a pastime for a quartet of Highlands children, three boys and a girl. We were well-behaved, exceptional in school, never late for dinner, and we never talked back to adults. And these balls were neglected, abandoned, essentially rubbish. But collecting these balls required climbing a five foot fence, a transgressive adventure for well-behaved children who were just three feet tall. We collected them like other children collected marbles or stamps.

I spotted a two-tone ball, half silver and half black. When I clambered back over the fence I saw my friends running in opposite directions, and why. Two White officers. "Get over here," the taller policemen said, "and empty your pockets!" I pulled them inside out. I had fifty cents. The blonde cop kept my prize find, my crescent moon ball, while his partner pocketed two others and opened the back door of the cruiser. I crawled inside.

"You know where we're going?" He didn't wait for me to answer. "We're gonna drive around until we find every one of your niglet friends, and all of youse are gonna apologize to every golfer in the park for stealin' their golf balls."

His shorter, darker sidekick laughed loudly. He was equally frightening. At least the air- conditioning was on. We drove swiftly through the park's winding roads but found no suspects. He angrily continued his dragnet. After three times around the park's winding roads we stopped near a fieldhouse. They exited the squad car, doors thudding together, engine quieted, air-conditioning off. I was locked inside. The groundskeeper, an older colored man, shook his head and pointed to the shrubbery. He was landscaping; besides, the park was full of children. The fieldhouse with Men and Women marked over arched doorways wasn't twenty feet away. The car was growing hotter and the groundskeeper continued to shake his head. My bladder was straining. I was afraid to pound on the window. Officer Laughter glided his finger across the horizon, as if hordes of wicked children were an approaching, golf ball-stealing army. Officer Blonde kept his right hand on his hip, near his pistol. Naked sunlight filled the car and a trickle of urine escaped, spreading darkly on my khaki trousers. I knocked on the window, softly at first, but as urine began to trickle down my leg I pounded more frantically. They glared sharply at me, then turned away again. I pounded harder on the window and screamed that they should let me out, my forehead beading with sweat. Officer Blonde stormed over, opened the door shouting, but seeing my darkening khakis he roughly yanked me out. It was too late. Not halfway to the fieldhouse I released a deluge down both legs. I stood still, crying, my khakis two-toned by piss, looking as if I were wearing chaps. I heard their car drive away. I trudged to a field house urinal, but I had nothing left to feed it. My mother would not believe me. She would call me a big baby. So I decided to cover my big baby pants-wetting shame with a big boy lie. I would prove I was a big boy who got into big boy trouble. I was near the West Lagoon. I waded in chest deep to cleanse my shame. I sank halfway up my shins in the sucking muddy bottom, my future university behind me, then struggled back to shore and trudged soggily, muddily home, wearing a single sneaker. My mother screamed curses at me when I arrived on the back porch. I was an anchor restraining her from an unencumbered life, like the one my father was enjoying with his younger, paler wife. I didn't tell her about the police car because she worked for the police.

As I watched the fat policemen, sleeping soundly, wondering if he did become distressed, would I rush to his aid? Or would I simply take one of the ratty pillows and place it firmly over his face. I stood silent in the room with my fat snoring policeman, watching over him, trapped like an embittered mother burdened with an unwanted child.

# BLACK BY UNPOPULAR DEMAND

By K. E. Mullins

For those of you that didn't get the memo. I was born this way. Skin stands the test of time and comes back again. I've been judged by my mere appearance. Dark, black, and beautiful. I wonder sometimes. Is that why he killed Sandra Bland? She towered over him like the queen she was or I am.

New form of lynching...cop killing

George Floyd – Knee in neck - 8:46

Ahmad Abrey – Running

Rayshard Brooks – Fell asleep in drive-thru – Atlanta

Daniel Prude – mental health episode, running naked, asphyxia – NY

Breonna Taylor – No knock warrant, wrong house

Atatiana Jefferson – killed by police in her home in front of eight-year-old nephew

Aura Rosser – domestic incident, tased and shot.

Stephon Clark – shot over 20 times, thought he was holding a gun. Holding a phone.

Botham Jean – shot by off-duty officer believing he was an intruder in her home. She was at wrong address/apt

Philando Castillo – shot in a traffic stop after saying he had a legal firearm with girlfriend and four-year-old in car.

This is the short version. The list is longer and continues to grow.

From my mere existence at the young age of grade school. I was told by another girl my same age that my skin always looked dirty. Yet, hers was clean. Lilly white it seemed. When does racism start? Apparently, it's taught. Very young. This was the early seventies.

Time would pass. I remember all too well. Declaring my independence from my mom and going shopping in a lil boutique. Hoping to find some new threads to wear. I declare. What I found was a shadow. Yes, a shadow mind you. Not my own. It followed me like my own. But closer, yet, not to close.

It was close enough to stare, not care. Close enough to observe and excuse, but it didn't dare. Until, they had motive. Neither of which I gave.

Did I call them on their actions? Of course, I did. My future encounters with them would be reverse. I'd throw them under the bus. It went something like this. I'd literally just put my foot in the store and the white women would ask, "May I help you?"

My response, terse. "No. I just walked in the store. Can I get a moment to look around?"

I know what you're thinking. I'm now the angry black woman. Contrar. I'm just the brown skinned woman trying to look around. What ya'll need to be looking at is the little white woman in the corner that's over there shoplifting. Of course, you're not paying her any never mind. "Why? 'Cause, she's white. She wouldn't do that.

Living while black is like living with a death sentence not carried out. I moved to California a few years after the Rodney King beating and for some reason, I thought California wasn't a racist state. I was attending school there while in the Navy. I was just coming home from a store. It was dark. I wasn't familiar with the neighborhood. So, I made a left instead of a right. No one was coming. The road appeared to be clear. Well, Murphy would have it. No sooner than I got to the traffic light, my rearview mirror lit up with blue lights. My exact words, "Where the hell did, he come from?" It was almost like that cop fell out the sky.

Of course, it's dark as crap where he wants me to pull over. I drive a little further.

He pulls out the bullhorn. "Stop the vehicle."

Like R Kelly said, "My mind is telling me no." So... I stop under a streetlight. It's perfect. For the life of me, I don't see the reason for all the flash and circumstance with a minor traffic violation. My palms are sweaty as he approaches the car. He comes to the window and ask the rhetorical question. "Do you know why I pulled you over?"

I respond, "No." Knowing full well it was because of an illegal turn. My thoughts were just give me the ticket and keep it moving.

"Well, did you see that no left turn sign?" he continues.

"No... I didn't. I'm not from here." I'm sure he could see my Florida tag, but I didn't say that.

"Well, you have a moving violation. Did you not see me behind you?" he ask.

"I did. But it was dark. So, I wanted to pull over under the light."

He stares into the car as if he wants to choke me out. "License and registration please."

I give license, registration, and military Id. He stares at my id for a moment and hands it back. In the meantime, he walks to his vehicle. Another patrol car pulls up behind him and yet, another. I'm thinking, really. This is what we're doing. There is not going to be no Rodney King going on here tonight. For a traffic violation. Come on....

Deputy dog comes back to the car... leaning on the side. "Here's a list of places you can go for driver improvement classes. This way you don't have any points against your license."

"Huh? What are you talking about?"

"These are places for you to go so your insurance won't increase?" he continues.

I'm thinking... I don't give a fuck about that. I want to leave. Who does this? I respond. "Ok. Not interested."

He looks puzzled and reluctantly hands me my license and the ticket. He replies. "You're free to go now."

Free to go? I say to myself. "Thanks." I reply. I look out my rearview mirror as he walks back to his cruiser. I pull off. The butterflies have now taken flight from my stomach. Thirty minutes passed over some bullshit turn. ONLY IN AMERICA.

ONLY IN AMERICA. Can I walk into a Denny's and get my food close to an hour later. Yeah, I said it, and this wasn't 1960s. This was in the 90s. I know what you're thinking. That's not true. If I could turn back the hand of time and you could walk in my skin, you'd see too.

It happened every time. No matter where the location. We'd come to Denny's after a night of partying. In good spirits. Civilized. That needs to be noted, 'cause for some reason people think we aren't. Any who, we'd be seated and let's just say for kicks. Another group of Caucasians males or females came in after us, say ten minutes later.

It never failed... they would always get their food before us. Astonished, I'd ask what's the hold up and get the same tired excuses. 'Y'all food is coming up. Or it's taking a little longer than expected,' etc. Finally, our food is in front of us. We're hungry, tired, and ready to eat. We take the first bite and the damn food is cold.

Now, being the human I am. I decided to try something else. It couldn't be possible that we've waited over an hour and the food is cold. Something must be wrong. I take a bite of my sausage this time. Same result. Before I can say, it. I hear across from me, "This is some bullshit."

I look into one of my friend's eyes and he's experiencing the same problem. Everyone is. We all come to the same conclusion and summoned the waitress. She listens but has a smirk on her face when she says, "It just came out. It can't be cold."

It is and they send it back. I decided not to. It took too long and I'm not trusting the results of them sending it back. These incidents would continue across Denny's in the South until a class action case is filed against them. I remember looking at the group across from us enjoying their food. They received long ago. It felt as we went back in time. Only this time, they let us in. However, if you think about it. It been better if they'd not served us. Cause this wasn't service.

ONLY IN AMERICA I can be prosecuted for the skin I'm in. I was born this way and by no means will I change it for another color. My roots are deep and my blood red. Red with rage and terror from those who call themselves American.

However, they are the aliens. Conquering and taking what doesn't belong to them. Intimidated by what is different. Killing what they can't accept or fail to.

Breathing while Black

It's always been a crime.

Let me put my ego over to the side.

I knew naught the word or the expletive I would hear.

In the new millennium, this is what they do. Pursue. Abuse. Yet, their supporters ridicule. Turn aside. In pride. Another son, brother, father, daughter, wife or mother dies. All put aside. We're of no value. Then or now.

Are we still wearing a mask? Figuring out the contrast, between us and them. Or are we still raisins in the sun? Hoping a new day will come in this time we're in.

I'd like to surmise we are neither, BUT a beautiful people. Put together among good and evil. We're equal. Educated. Creative. Unstoppable. We are their beginning and the end. Don't you remember Pharaoh and his friend. In the land of Egypt, the place where God stopped the evil. To free his people.

Now, if you're wondering those were all people of color. I discover. This is a plot. Some say yeah, others not.

Systemic

Nigga in a passing, all day wondering why.

# FIRESTORM

By Antonio David Lyons

*Mary Fitzgerald Square, Newtown Cultural Precinct, Johannesburg, South Africa. Out of the darkness establishing shots of surrounding institutions: Market Theater, Museum Africa, Kaldi's, N1 Highway, Murals. Crowd shots are projected on a screen. The performance is larger than life. Street Theatre.*

*Lights are used to simulate an inferno. The performer stands center stage.*

I won't be silent anymore as a firestorm swirls around me

An inferno seeking to consume my soul and my identity.

My manhood, the fuel feeding the flames as they rage out of control.

The fire brigade stands with arms folded as timbers of my soul turn to ash.

I gaze through molten tears, a cage of hurt and disbelief and rage and misery at my plight

Who started this fire that ravages me inside out?

What accelerant was poured across my slumbering form just before the match was cast upon me?

Nowhere to turn to for relief. The heat peels the skin from my flesh and tears the meat from my bones in crispy blackened strips.

I blaze like a beacon on a hill drawing to me those that love the macabre or mask sympathy in fast moistening downcast eyes.

Like moths to a flame they come.

There are those that come to bear witness... so they can speak of this moment to future generations.

It is to them my liquid eyes turn... I try to speak, but my boiled tongue can no longer articulate... I speak with a look, " I am not the first or the last, I am one of many… turn your gaze upon this world… cast your sight across the land and see… see with the fullness of yourself… don't be blinded by limited sight… we count in the millions that burn silently, brightly and completely.

We burn hoping you will lend a hand to dose these flames that destroy so much… too much.

And a shed tear hisses and evaporates on its way to the scorched earth at my feet, too little moisture to ease my pain.

I exhale and let go… consumed entirely… unto death.

ashes to the wind carry me far and wide

I lived for love

As do many of my brothers

*Stage hands carry the performer off the stage.*

BLACKOUT

# THE REAPERS ON WOODBROOK AVENUE

By Mardee Bennett

*TAMAR - Late 40s, Black, Corey's mother, Managing Director of an investment firm.*

**TAMAR:** (controlled; brisk) You need to take responsibility for yourself. Your behavior. You're the grown man standing here buck-ass-naked. I've known men like you before. I've seen what they're capable of. And what they get away with. For what (finding the word) conceivable reason did you invite my son into your home? Why were you lying naked on that table? So many questions. Didn't you see what kind of state he was in? You have eyes. Or have you been blinded by your own desperation? Maybe you are that loathsome. You chose to ignore what was in front of you. To not call his mother. To not call his father. To not inquire. Instead you turned a gun on him. Because you were frightened you say. So, what. You should have known better. You're an elder. This is supposed to be a community. The elders are supposed to look after the children. But you see Mr. Reaper, I know there are predators in the world. There are people who do not want young, black men to succeed. There are people who will do everything in their power to see black men fail. You enjoy young, black boys, hmm? I see that. You use them as if they're... things. Enjoy them like I enjoy a good game of golf. Every now and then. On Saturdays. You call one over. Pay them. You keep it quiet. You don't have a problem. You go on telling yourself that. I know you. I know how y'all operate. Will you ever be held accountable? Will you? No, no. We can't have that. You're white. And a man. Go on destroying black lives. Your ancestors did. After all, it's in your nature—the desire to destroy us. Whip us. Rape us. Lynch us. Shoot us. Steal our land. Send dogs after us. Burn down the village—whatever it takes to insure we do not prosper.

# THE SIGNING

By Sharon Cleveland Blount

*ROBERT HEMINGS, 32, mulatto, well-tailored, right hand missing. Former personal assistant to Thomas Jefferson.*

**ROBERT:** I remember all too well setting my eyes upon those words etched on the parchment, "that all men are created equal... endowed by their Creator with certain unalienable Rights... Life, Liberty and the Pursuit of Happiness." (beat)

A swelling of goodness, even pride for the colonies, arose in me, from somewhere deep inside myself. (beat)

That night, like usual, I went into the study to blow out the candles after you retired. The parchment lay sprawled across the desk, the ink needing more time to dry. The heavy smell of iron, mixed in the black ink, filled the air. The quill and ink I brought back from Mason's print shop, sat in the carrier. When you sent me to town, days before, to pick it up, you indicated it would be used for an important signing. That's what you told me. I knew to be careful with the quill. It was exquisite, made with a long, white, swan's feather, a delicate instrument chosen for such a heavy purpose. I was proud, like you said I should be, to be the carrier of the quill. I hesitated as I approached the parchment. My curiosity was peaked. My eyes laid upon the letters, superbly shaped, spelling, "All men are created equal." There was no 'but' or 'except' that followed. A significant, black dot powerfully ended the sentence. Period.

I felt a nervousness I don't recall ever feeling before, a trembling in my being. Somehow, I sensed the magnitude of what lay before me. I fixed my eyes on the parchment. Again, I looked over the letters that formed the words, "...Life, Liberty and the Pursuit of Happiness." My heart jumped with joy. Could this be? Could I now have this Liberty, my Freedom? In this America? Would I be allowed to speak up for myself, and my family? Would those who have been silenced, enslaved, be heard, be in control of their own lives? Be protected? Justly treated? Allowed to live free? These thoughts bombarded my mind. I turned away. My stomach churned with intense anticipation. (beat)

That night, I tossed and turned, eager, yet agonizing over the words my eyes had read. (beat)

As we walked along the street the next day, heading to Independence Hall, you proudly carried the rolled parchment, bound with the thin leather string that I meticulously measured, cut and tied.

It was signing day. Instead of walking my usual three steps behind, I picked up my pace to walk alongside you, empowered by your words written on the parchment. (beat)

You stopped.

Stood.

Silent.

Your eyes cut into me, sharper than a sword piercing my heart, with more force than any captured slave beating I had witnessed. (beat)

I stepped back, resumed my usual place. (beat)

How could I be so foolish... to think... that I was included? A black boy. (beat)

I entered the Hall, astutely dressed in my skin, representing the condemned black male. The quill and ink that I carried would be used to omit enslaved people from receiving "Liberty, and the Pursuit of Happiness." Leaving us still reaching for equality--freedom.

It was you, who allowed, in fact, insisted, I learn to read. When you reached for the quill, your eyes met mine. You recognized that I read and understood the empowering words written so boldly on the parchment. Your quick glance away told me you knew the full gravity of what this quill and ink would do to people like me, to my family. My eyes fixed on your every gesture, your every move. You hesitated, even gazed back at me. My eyes hung on you, like strange fruit, yet you dipped into the ink and pressed the quill to the parchment. On a silver tray, I presented the quill, with ink, to each signer. I stared as each lifted the quill to dip in the ink and sign. I wanted to be seen, recognized, to be included in the liberating words, to be equal. Do I dare ask, "Does this include me?"

How does one sign, in agreement, to the all-inclusive words, while at the same time denying ME the right to them? ALL MEN, not some, ALL men, including ME, A MALE among ALL men, should be included. Yet, I wasn't even considered, even as I stood carrying the white swan's feather quill, its position regarded more than me. (beat)

You see me, yet you don't. I am aware of my right to belong, to exist in this land. I am created equal, yet you fail to see. I am entitled to every word you sign. You cannot sign me out. You just signed me in.

# EPICENTER

By Zachariah Ezer

**LAMAR:**

When, in the seven years that we've known each other, have you ever heard me say the word 'nigger'?

*beat*

Exactly, because I would never say it around you. That's not how this friendship works. I can see immediately how uncomfortable it makes you. I keep the part of me that's Black far away from you guys. I know you're not interested.

*beat*

Say whatever you want about Alex, but at least he understands that. I've been hanging out with you a lot more lately, but I'm tired of suppressing parts of myself just to feel like I can exist.

*beat*

And my mom isn't any fucking better. She's the picture of dignified, obsessed with looking so presentable that a white person couldn't possibly find anything to object to. Owns a law firm, deacon at the church, kid headed Up North.

*beat*

You know she
makes me read Langston Hughes every summer? I fucking hate Langston Hughes. "They'll see how beautiful we are and be ashamed." Unlikely. She's got me on that same track, but I'm not doing it. Fuck, Kevin. You want to leave home to be a better member of your family? I want to go because the whole world can't be like mine. It can't. I am dying to go into the fucking epicenter of Blackness because at least one person there is going to understand me.

*beat*

They have to.

# reconstructing whiteness

by Alva Rogers
(Monologue from *the life before/ reconstruction/ reconstructing whiteness*)

LIGHTS-UP ON MOTHER

**MOTHER**
in the dream
she wipes the rain from her eyes
and
she runs and runs to get home to meet her husband and baby
and
everything is dead:
the house is dead
the father is dead
the baby is dead
everything is dead
then
eden
a different kind of eden
there are no apples and no trees
ignorance is bliss
no sky
no sea blue green sea
no moon or stars to dream upon
no sun to keep them warm

according to the book

once upon a time
there was another eden
a man and a woman lived there
according to the book
it was above ground
it was an above ground garden
according to the book

books hold history
stories of the life before
which is why they are no longer in this time of reconstruction
where you are
ignorance is bliss
where you are
when I was a girl
like you
the world was different
yet the same
the purest ones continued to rule
numbers of people of color
had quadrupled
and
pure rulers
(those without color as they were known then)
were paying their daughters to lie in birthing beds
as you lie in yours
it was their view
that their race was dying
as people of all colors
brown, red, yellow
even those without color
began loving each other
marrying each other
having babies
and mixing into one color
and it was decided
that a division would be made
all people without color
would live
above
with the sun, moon and stars
and
all the colored peoples
would live below
without sky
without wind

no moon or stars to dream upon
no sun to keep them warm

I am in Eden
the above ground Eden where I have returned
to my purest state of heart, spirit and soul
the book says
we are all children above the clouds
and I am sad to know
the tears we shed for those we miss below
fall as raindrops that you will never know
after the division
all the parents of all children of color were eradicated
therefore
eradicating all knowledge of the life before reconstruction
eradicating all knowledge of people of all colors
brown, red, yellow
and those without color
loving each other
marrying each other
having babies
and mixing into one color.

before my elimination
an exterminator said:
elimination is necessary to preserve your race.
to preserve and make
your color and all colors pure again.
no, I said
you speak not the truth
you do not want to make brown, red, yellow pure again you want
to
re-create...
re-build...
no
you want to... reconstruct...
people/

08:46

without color
you want to
reconstruct:
reconstruct
whiteness

LIGHTS OUT

# ANTIGONE'S MONOLOGUE

By Marie Mayingi

**ANTIGONE:** I've always thought of my country and my people as this incredibly rich and colourful blend of origins, cultures and traditions. I was raised in a very cosmopolitan neighbourhood. It felt like a strength. My horizons were as broad as they could possibly be. I grew up hearing languages from every continent, tasting food from all over the globe, without ever leaving home. It felt like being part of a huge family. When I was a kid, I couldn't see further than that... I remember it being a game to us, as children. We'd taunt the cops who patrolled in our neighbourhood, we'd curse at them and throw rocks at their cars. We knew they hated us and we were supposed to hate them too, but we didn't know why.

We didn't even know why they were there in the first place, but they were part of our everyday life.

As I got older, I realized it wasn't a game. It had never been one. They were the state's minions, who were specifically asked to keep the "ghetto" in order. We were nothing but an evil they had their colonizer ancestors to blame for.

Being confronted with constant marginalization made us stronger, though. We had to become one.

And now we're being antagonized because we refuse to be silenced, we refuse to let bandits with badges spread fear.

As a black woman, as the sister of men who were murdered because of their colour and upbringing, I feel like an enemy of my own nation. But I refuse to let them corrupt my land.

# THE VOICE INSIDE MY HEAD

By Louis D. Johnson

*The curtain rises. We're in the semi-darkened chapel of St. Benedict's Episcopal Church in Boston's Mattapan neighborhood. On a long, flag-draped conference table at the front of the room are several framed pictures of a young Black man. A giant white poster board with various ribbons and other sports memorabilia sits in the center of the table. To the left of the poster, a number of football and basketball trophies stand. The lights in the room flicker. The room goes dark. Out of the darkness, a MAN-IN-BLACK appears. The lights flicker on, but they're very dim. The Man-in-Black looks at all the stuff on the table; he picks up one of the ribbons. He places it back on the table.*

**MAN-IN-BLACK:** Good evening, everybody. I know you're wondering what's goin' on here. Well, the church is havin' a memorial service. For me... If you're confused, don't worry, I'll explain at all, later. First, let me take a look at these pictures.

*MAN-IN-BLACK picks up one of the framed pictures.*

(*holding a picture*) This is me in my younger days... When I still had hair!

*MAN-IN-BLACK laughs. He places the picture back on the table; he picks up another picture.*

And this is me back when I was in the military. Man, I hated the fuckin' military! Nothin' but a bunch of racist pricks, yellin' at me all the damn time.

*MAN-IN-BLACK places the picture back on the table. He picks up a trophy; he reads its inscription.*

(*reading the trophy*) First place, 100yd dash, All-City Track Meet, Boston!

*MAN-IN-BLACK places the trophy back on the table.*

Man, what a day that was! Christ, I can't believe how fast I was back then! Anyway, like I was sayin', for what it's worth, you're here to attend my memorial service. See, last week, while I was out on my morning run, I was shot and killed. By a freakin' cop! Now I know what you're thinkin', 'What did he do?' Or you're probably sayin' to yourself, 'He musta done something'. But you're wrong. I didn't do nothin'! I was out on my run — like I do every mornin' — and this asshole shoots me. For nothin'! What surprises me the most about all of it is that since I got shot, the shit has gotten crazy as Hell! I mean, there're riots all over the place, people marchin', demanding justice, doin' all kinds of shit in my name. When it first started, I thought it was cool, but now, with all the lootin' and stuff... (s*hrugs*) I don't know... But, hey, that's not why I'm here. I'm here 'cause there are a lot of people out there who think I got what I deserved. Well, I'm here to tell ya', I didn't deserve that! And damn what you saw on TV, on Facebook, or wherever the fuck you saw it! That is not how it went down, and, no, I didn't deserve what happened to me! So, to clear shit up, once and for all, I'm goin' to tell you what <u>really</u> went down, and you decide for yourself whether I deserved to be shot in the back, or not. Like I said earlier, I was on my morning run when I saw this cop car drive past me. Hey, I was jogging, minding my own business, so I didn't think nothin' of it. I mean, I'd been doin' this same run, at the same time, every morning for the last ten years. All the cops in the neighborhood knew me — a lot of 'em by name! — 'cause I joked around wit' 'em when I saw 'em in Dunkin' Donuts when I went in to get my daily shot of espresso. Anyway, when the cop drove past me the second time, and started slowin' down, I got a little nervous. So I slowed down, too. When he saw that, he immediately turned around and flipped on his blues. I watched him leap out of the cruiser — pistol in hand! — and I knew the shit was on! "Show me your hands," the white cop yelled, his sidearm pointed directly at my face. For some reason, even with the gun in my face, I wasn't afraid. Not at first, anyway. I hadn't done anything wrong, so why should I be afraid? I kept tellin' myself to relax — that it would be over in a minute — but, hard as I tried, I could not relax. How <u>can</u> you relax with a cocked nine millimeter pointed at your head? "Show me your goddamn hands!" the policeman screamed a second time. I tried to put up my hands, but I wasn't puttin' 'em up fast enough. So he clocked me upside the head with the barrel of his pistol, sending me sprawling to the pavement. Lying there, blood gushing from my head, I was now completely terrified. I had to get away, but I was too scared to run. I knew that that if I tried to run, and he caught me, he would kill me for sure. So I lay there, on the steaming hot asphalt, his size 13 police boot firmly planted at the base of my skull. "I got you now, nigger" he taunted as he ground his boot into my neck. I heard his walkie-talkie go off, and the moment he went to answer it, he raised his foot off my back. That was the break I was lookin' for! When the voice in my head yelled, "RUN," I leaped off the ground and took off running. That was the worst mistake of my life. I was a few feet away from him when I heard the shot. Then I felt the flame. Do you know what it feels like to get shot? It feels like someone's stabbin' you with a red-hot poker — over and over and over again. I grabbed my arm and I could feel the warm blood oozing through my fingers. I realized I'd been hit, but I tried not to panic; I knew that if I panicked, it was over. I tried to run faster. That's when I heard the second shot. I think it hit me in the leg, but I really can't remember. Probably 'cause it didn't hurt as bad as the first shot. Or maybe I was too scared to feel it. "Stop nigger, stop," I heard him yell, seconds before the third shot hit me in the lower part of my back droppin' me to the pavement. As I lay there, sprawled on my back, in the convenience store parking lot, I could hear the sound of his boots running toward me. I was in excruciating pain. All I could feel was burning. My whole body was on fire! I started gettin' woozy. Before I blacked out, I looked around, and I realized that there were people everywhere. Watching me... Dying... As the cop walked closer, everything went black. Slowly, I felt the contents of my body spillin' out of me. Shit, piss, blood, everything, pourin' out, onto the street for the whole world to see — on Facebook Live and Instagram! With the crowd staring on, the cop stood over me, his weapon in one hand, his walkie-talkie in the other. All of a sudden, I started hearing sirens. I was completely out of it when the paramedics finally got me on the stretcher. As they ripped off my shirt, to reveal my wounds, all I could think was, "God, help me, please! I can't fuckin' breathe!"

# SPIT

By Diana Mucci

I grew up on the south side of Chicago, somewhere between the Blacks on the East and the Whites on the West. I was happy in between. It was safe, friendly and a whole lot of fun. In the winter, after the first big snowfall, we'd make snow angels, have snowball fights and play lost in the wilderness. In the summer, we'd ride our bikes, jump rope and have family picnics in the park. But things were changing and before we knew it, teenagers sprouted on every corner and with teenagers came gangs, graffiti, boom boxes and daytime parties.

Dad didn't like it and everyone heard about it. "Kids, one day we're going to the West, where the grass is greener and the people Whiter. No Rif-Raf out West. Smart people. Hardworking. Classy. That's where we belong, kids. Why do you think I'm not home much? Cuz I'm busting my ass working two jobs to get us there, that's why!! But don't you worry, kids. We're gonna make it out West. You better believe, we're gonna make it."

I must've heard him say that every single day, until one morning without a word, Mami, Dad, my Haitian grandmother, Poupee with her stolen grocery cart from Jewel, my four sisters and Sparky, our little horn-dog of a Chihuahua, packed our bags and took off.

We made it to the West alright - a whole four blocks west. We could've carried our furniture and walked there but we drove instead, and within 5 minutes we pulled into the driveway. My heart raced a bit from the excitement of seeing this quaint house that looked much like the one we just left. I almost ran toward it, but Dad headed for the other house – the one that was slightly slanted to the left. It was a yellow frame house with missing parts, like the staircase, half the porch and some of the roof.

But Dad was right. The grass was greener here. People spent days and nights watering, planting, weeding, trimming, mowing and mulching. Our next-door neighbor, Mr. Svenski, won the contest for having the greenest grass and for his invention of an electric barb-wired fence that would fry kids who came within five inches of it. I got caught in it once.

We were playing catch on the 2 x 2 sidewalk Dad had marked off for us at the foot of the porch. I hit the ball to my sister, but not being very good at aiming, I hit the ball smack in the middle of Mr. Svenski's luscious, super-duper, green lawn and it had just been watered. Without thinking, I ran to get it and my foot got caught on the wire on my way out. I swear it fried my hair! Poof! Big Hair. Big Haitian hair.

"Diabla!" Mami shouted her favorite nickname for me, devil. Mami was a beautiful White Puerto-Rican with perfectly straight hair. She didn't speak English and didn't know what to do with my suddenly tightly-wound Haitian curls. She tried brushing it frantically, but it only got bigger.

"Ouch!" I screamed.

She pulled harder. "Toma, por ser tan estúpida!" She was right. I deserved it. I was sooo stupid. Why did I have to step on his grass, anyway? Those White people were smart. Real smart.

The night before the first day of school, I was so beside myself giddy, I couldn't sleep. The eve before every first day of school was always like Christmas Eve to me, except I wouldn't check the presents under the tree. I'd get up in the middle of the night to do inventory on my school stuff. Shiny shoes, check. White socks, check. Polyester uniform, check. Backpack, check. Lunch box, check. I'd sniff my new crayons, my fresh notebooks, my loose-leaf paper, my erasers, my #2 pencils and my glue. Hmmm, that Elmer's glue.

But this particular eve of first days of school must have been the best of them all. I felt the flutter of butterflies and fell in and out of consciousness, dreaming about my graffiti-free school, my smart and pretty teacher and my cool, White friends. In the morning, Mami made the usual oatmeal, slightly burnt. "Comenselo, despreciadas!!" We ate it fast, so as not to seem ungrateful.

"Bye, Mami! We gave her our usual hug and kiss.

“Bye, Poupee!” Poupee sat on the front porch enjoying her Café Bustelo and Camel cigarette. She put out the cigarette quickly, so she could grab my face and kiss it. Then she gave me such an embrace that it fueled me.

“Bonne chance, Nana,” she wished me good luck in French. My grandmother had been living with us on and off since I was born and I had learned to speak a little French and Creole over the years. By age twelve however, I settled for English, “Thank you, Poupee! Love you!”

“Bye, Sparky!” I kicked the horn-dog off my leg.

Dad waited for us at the bottom of the stairs. “See that,” he pointed proudly down the street. “Look at all those kids waiting to walk with you. What did I tell you? Smart. Classy people.”

He was right. There must have been ten of them, mostly boys, waiting for us on the corner. Oh, yeah! Life in the West was getting better already! Huge smiles. Laughter. Cheering. I knew at least one of them would like me.

“Hi,” I had a smile from ear to ear. He was tall, blonde, blue-eyed and beautiful.

SPIT! SPLAT!

My heart was in my hand when I realized he spit on my right shoulder.

"Spics!"

“What’s a Spic?” I asked my sister, Lisa.

“Spic ‘n Span, stupid!” she didn’t look convinced. “You know, like we’re all clean and shiny.”

“Go back where you came from, you dirty Spics!”

Well, there went that theory.

SPIT. SPLAT.

One landed on my shiny, new shoes.

"What do you mean go back where we came from?" I shouted in my head. "It's a few blocks that way!"

SPIT. SPLAT.

And another landed on my big hair.

"Smelly Spics!"

"Hey, we don't smell!" I shouted louder to myself.

SPIT. SPLAT.

Right on my face.

"Lisa, tell them something," I whispered, desperate, terrified, angry and confused.

"No. Keep your head down. Don't look them in the eye. Stay together. Closer. Hold hands. Tighter," Lisa was resolved in her terror.

"Nigger Spics!

It didn't take long to realize what Spic meant. It wasn't clean and shiny. Spics were ugly, despicable and unthinkable humans.

SPIT. SPIT. SPIT. SPIT. SPIT. SPIT. SPIT.

All the way to school. No. Church. You had to go to mass every morning to start the day right. I suppose it was to confess after you SPIT. I remember Father Patrick's sermon about a fresh start. I only remember it because that's all I could think about. All. Day. Long.

Fresh start. Fresh start.

How could I be fresh, when I wreaked of SPIT? And that pretty teacher I dreamt about that night turned out to be a stout, red-nosed, angry nun with black-rimmed glasses and bad breath.

"So, you're the new girl. How do you like it here?" Sister Judith asked me in front of the whole class, who was already mumbling and snickering.

"It's OK, I guess." I twirled a few strands of my curly hair.

"Speak up, Missy! Oh. You don't speak English, do you?

"No. I mean, yes. Of course, I speak English." I twirled tighter.

"I hear your mother is from another country, Mexico, right?" Her nose flared when she talked.

"No. My mother's from Puerto Rico." I twirled so tight that a few strands tore off.

"Well, you're all the same to me."

"No, I don't think we're all the same." I let the loose strands fall to the ground.

"Don't you get sassy with me, Missy!" By now, she had made her way to my desk and pointed her twisted finger between my eyes.

"I'm putting you in our remedial reading group with . . ."

"With who?" I thought. "The kids that SPIT? But I read better. I read faster. Listen to them. They can't read. They only know how to SPIT."

SPIT. SPIT. SPIT. SPIT. SPIT. SPIT. SPIT. SPIT. SPIT.

They SPIT. Every. Single. Day. It was like that out West. No Rif-Raf. Smarter. Classier. Whiter. I guess they liked to SPIT. I didn't like it. We never SPIT. No one SPIT back home.

About six months later, I earned my way out of the remedial reading group and finally had a few friends. One day, out of the blue, just like that - no more SPIT. Not a drop.

Oh God! One of them liked me! Ken Swade, that tall, blonde, blue-eyed babe. He liked me?

"I like you," he said. "You're not like the rest of them,"

"Thank you?" I couldn't believe what I was hearing.

"Yea. No problem. So, will you go out with me?" He brushed his shiny, blonde hair away from his eyes. Gosh, he was something.

"I don't know," I answered. "I need to think about it."

It took me a whole two seconds. Thanks, but no thanks, loser.

"Ken, we're so wrong for each other. You see, you like to SPIT and I don't. I think it's a disgusting habit and you think it's cool. I think it makes you weak, and you swear it makes you strong."

That's what I wanted to tell him. I wanted to hurt him with my words, to make him feel as small as he had made me feel once. But I thought it would only make me pathetic, just like him. So instead, I said, "My parents won't let me."

"Why? That's dumb." He had a way with words, that one.

"Well, they're old-fashioned and think thirteen is kind of young. I'm sorry." I lied. I wasn't sorry.

His jaw dropped, mouth wide open. I don't think anyone had ever said 'no' to him before. I saw some SPIT drip onto his chin. I didn't say anything. I let him sit with it. All wet and smelly. I imagined it dripping onto his torn t-shirt and soaking his jeans down to his dirty shoes. I wondered for just one second, how he might've felt if I had poured that SPIT all over him. And then I smiled and without another word, I walked away. Proud. Not because of the feeling that sweet revenge sometimes gives, but because I didn't care if he liked me anymore. It didn't matter. It would never matter again. I had arrived and I thanked him for it. I thanked every single one of them because their SPIT made me a stronger person. Made me Classier. Smarter.

Dad was right when he said we were going to make it out West. We did make it. We made it big.

# I DIDN'T RAISE MY SON TO DIE

By Sharnell Blevins

*AT RISE: Street. Mid-morning. A young Black man is laying on the ground center stage. A semi- circle of people are standing around, including two police officers slightly away from the crowd in bewilderment.*

*MARY runs into the scene from stage right, sitting down and placing the head of the young man unto her lap.*

MARY: Son . . . Son . . . Momma's here . . . Momma's here . . . stand back, stand back . . . no . . . no, no , no body need to do nothing to my baby . . . he alright . . . he alright . . . come on now baby . . . John . . . John . . . Momma's here . . . Leti, go call an ambulance . . . go'on now call . . . call NOW . . . shit . . . take out your phone . . . dial . . . 9 . .. dial . . . you know the emergency number . . . oh God . . . NO . . . NO . . . John . . . Momma's here . . . Momma's here . . . I'm here . . . I 'm . . . no . . . no . . . he alright . . . call . . . he birth hesself yep . . . he sure did birth his own self . . . he want to be born right then didn't waste no time he said momma now I'm here Momma I'm here . . . did you call 'em . . . he burst out my womb ready for the world he wanted to be here he wanted to live . . . he wanted to be among us . . . he wasted no time neither he . . .they comin . . . okay . . . okay . . . I'm here Johnny . . . I'm here . . .remember you usedta snatch food off my plate and mushed it into your mouth . . . fingers covered in sweet potatoes . . . turning your fingers and mouth orange. . . your favorite . . . candied yams . . . never could tell no difference from yams to sweet potatoes . . . I never told you when I changed it up . . . they cook the same . . . seem like I slicing potatoes for days and days . . . you never could get enough . . . I'm makin' some now . . . get up so I don't burn the ones on my stove . . . get up . . . I don't hear no sirens . . . did you call the damn ambulance . . . wake up baby wake up . . . what ya'll do to my baby Mr. Officer . . . whatcha do to my baby boy . . . come on John . . . get up . . . you took your first steps right over there in the park . . . threw you shoes . . . threw them out of that stroller . . . cried and cried until I took you out . . .come on baby wake up . . . told you I wasn't picking up after you no more . . . you must've believed me . . . you cried n' cried 'til I took you outta that stroller . . . you got the damn shoes you own self . . . you walked by yourself . . . I didn't even help . . . I was too stunned to stop him . . . he walking and all . . . my beautiful baby boy . . . Leti you call, you call . . officer you call, you called didn't you . . . he left 'fore I got up . . . that's my Pepsi rolling to gutter . . . I'ma sure he got 'em from Gulliver's at the corner . . . you knows I love me some Pepsi . . . now baby you can't go to sleep here in the street open your eyes baby let's go in the house, open your eyes Johnny . . . JOHNNY! JOHNNY! WAKE UP! . . . no, no, no, you gotsa wake up . . . what cha doin' . . . you hear me, whatcha doin' . . . you ain't no ambulance people . . . you gone called your friends officer . . . we need an ambulance . . . get my baby to the hospital . . . Leti call for . . . call an ambulance . . . leave me alone . . . I'm not answering no questions . . . I gotta stay with my baby boy . . . he needs. . . he . . . CPR . . . he needs CPR STAT . . . CPR . . . NOOOOO! I DIDN'T RAISE MY SON TO DIE! NO! HELP HIM! HELP HIM! . . . help him . . . please . . .

*MARY continues speaking but in a whisper that only her son can hear.*

# A PARK FOR CHILDREN TO PRETEND IN

By Vincent Terrell Durham

**DARRYL:** Him— they—them—They killed our son. We moved to this neighborhood because we thought it was safe. Because it had a playground. Because it had a park. A park for our son to pretend in. Isn't twelve years old still being a child? Isn't this park where he was supposed to play? For him to use his imagination? Black boys pretend. Black boys play. He's allowed to be whatever it is he wanted to be inside this park. I never met a boy who didn't ask for a toy gun. Asking for one for his birthday, or just asking to be asking for something. Picking up a stick and pretending he had one. They made a Christmas movie about it. All about one boy wanting a BB gun. But my boy you shoot. My boy you think is something different. He was playing with a toy gun inside a park. A park for him to pretend in. He wasn't pretending to be nothing bad. He wasn't pretending to be nothing wrong. Look what's pinned to his chest. He drew it and I cut it out for him. It's big and yellow and sheriff is spelled out on it in big black magic marker. Didn't you see that? Didn't them cops who shot him see that? What did they see when they saw my son, because I see a twelve year old little boy. Why didn't they see that? Why didn't they see he still needed time to grow into his big ole' head? He's never going to get that chance. He's never going to grow into that big ole' head that he got from me. That I got from my daddy and he got from his daddy. He's never going to be able to give to his son because you shot him. You shot my son. You killed my boy inside a park. A park for children to pretend in.

# FOLLOW THE FIREFLIES

By Christian St. Croix

*Lights up on OUR NEW FRIEND, a man, Black, late teens/early 20s. A clearing in the middle of the woods. There's something strange about the trees. They're both calming and unsettling.*

*OUR NEW FRIEND is making conversation with us.*

**OUR NEW FRIEND:** Donny and I used to race each other. Go, go, go, you shoulda seen us! We were like bunnies! Dashing between the trees, climbing up on the branches. He left awhile back. Followed the fireflies out.

And Patrick! I called him Mister Patrick. Mister Patrick wasn't much for running, said his bones wouldn't make it. Fool old man, his bones were long in the dust. He could run just fine if he wanted to. He followed the fireflies too.

*He looks past us, nods.*

That's Miller over there. He was only a few years younger than me. He doesn't talk much, but he's always smiling.

They come to the grove, they go from the grove. I make friends with some of them. Some ain't so friendly, 'just wanna be left alone. Some are... sad. They're sad for a really long time. Like Little Barbara. See that stump over there? Little Barbara used to sit right there and just cry and cry. I'd say, "Get on up, Barbie Doll! Look at all the amazing things we can do here! Look how high we can jump! Look how fast we can run! Look at how tall the trees are!" She wouldn't take her eyes off her lap. She cried for her mother. She cried for the body she left behind. The fireflies came early for her. I think they took pity. She got up off that stump and followed them out. Didn't even look back.

We don't even know if it's a grove, we just call it that. There's trees that go on and on forever and up and up forever. There's a creek over that way, you can stick your feet in. Moss so soft, you'd swear you were standing on silk. And it's always night here, but not the kind of night you get lost in. There's no shadows to scare you here.

No bears, no gators, nothing to chase you. The grove ain't Heaven and it ain't Hell. It's...

*Struggles to find the words to describe it.*

...a place for us to rest, a place for us to come to ourselves, make peace with the way we... with what happened to us...

*A darkness falls over OUR NEW FRIEND's face. Something close to rage. The switch should be jarring.*

They took me out of my mama's house. I kicked and screamed. I fought, you hear me? Fought as hard as I could!

*A moment.*

I told them I didn't get fresh with the postmaster's daughter. I'd be a fool. Any colored boy would be a fool. I'd never said a single word to that gal. But she swore I made eyes at her. She said I blew a kiss.

*A moment.*

They dragged me into some old barn. I'm still there. Buried beneath the horses.

*He calms, forces a smile.*

Say, do you remember how you—?

*This seems to upset us.*

Hey. Hey. There ain't no shame. It's how we all got here. All of us. We all left too soon, fell at their hands. Hey. Hey. Okay. You don't have to talk about it. You just rest. We're meant to rest here. We're meant to run and dance and find peace. When we're ready, the fireflies will come for us. You're supposed to follow the fireflies out, you see. They'll lead you to The Better Place. I'm still waiting for mine.

*A glimmer of light falls on his face. He looks towards it, spots something in the distance and gasps.*

Look. Ain't they something? You see how pretty they are? All bright and twinkling like that? Did they—? They've come for Miller!

*Calls out, laughing.*

You go on, Miller! Go on and follow them! I'll see you real soon, boy! Go on, Miller!

*A moment as he watches Miller leave with the fireflies. Then quietly, happily, a longing smile.*

Go on.

# MONOLOGUE FOR A TUTTING FACE

By J. E. Robinson

*SETTING: Simple staging, with card table and a folding chair, on a bare stage. NEGRO MAMA II may enter or be seated, as she pleases.*

*NEGRO MAMA II carries a mask and a play script.*

**NEGRO MAMA II:** I would nod to you, if I could, do so and retain my dignity. But, alas, you are too slow to catch real life. You blink too much, staring at shadows on the wall and mistaking ceiling flecks for stars. It serves little purpose to bash a donkey repeatedly with a two-by-four. After a few centuries, it becomes evident that the jackass either is dead or doesn't care. So, for this, I shall enter the cave with you and with you turn my back to reality, naturally. Make room on that couch, mama: yet another mask-wearer is here.

Negro Mama II. You know: that nosy neighbor that comes over and drinks coffee with Negro Mama I as the sirens from the Man go by. I got my own mask. See? It frowns and hums for me. "Umm, um! Lord, Lord!"

What? Them? For a splib from Central Casting, you got that white boy's naivete down pat. Ha! No, I'm not able to frown and hum on my own. Most plays' timing is off from real time. Especially if they try writing for us. I wouldn't know how to do it and stay with my agent. Having my own mask, it means I can frown and hum and moan and cry and drink coffee and still make next month's rent. If Butterfly McQueen and Stepin Fetchit could do it, Negro Mama II from Central Casting can do it, too. Negro Mama II just got to look like she's all "my feets tired" when she thrown down her lines. What mask do you got? Nice Smile.

Ain't you seen a mama on the couch play before? In this business, Negro Mama II got to move—they call it "jook"—with a whole lot of jazz. Negro Mama I got the Sister Rosetta Tharp going, but Negro Mama II got to get that Sarah Vaughn, Alberta Hunter, and Billie

Holliday all rolled up. Sassy and jazzy, they say, they say all the way. At least, that what my agent say. Keep that brat of his in an overpriced day care. Anyway, I was complimenting its smile, not yours, and not your eyes. Though, by smiling, you seem to say so. Never mind this book!

"Run lines?" What lines I got? All I got to do is hum "Lord, Lord," and "Um-Um" while fanning myself, sitting on the couch. That's what has happened to Negro Mama II after Hattie McDaniel went crying off with that Oscar. Ask Lorraine Hansberry. Old gal, she started it. She wasn't even in the grave when everyone started ripping off her Mama. "Chekhov?" This is the wrong book, baby. Hand me that other one. I do no Star Trek.

"August Wilson?" What call for Negro Mamas he got in August Wilson's plays? Forget Negro Mama II—ten plays... five Negro Mamas; count 'em—he ain't got no call for no Negro Mama II! "August Wilson?" A fool would starve holding her breath to be Negro Mama II in August Wilson! That what you want for me? You build a career as a Negro Mama II, go do Aristophanes! That's what you should do. You like eating? Never mind the salmon and filet mignon, I'm talking ground chuck and fish cakes. What you need a lawyer for? You need that supermarket, at the bottom of the hill! You're an artist—or call yourself an artist. A writer... well then, let me tell say something to you, baby: all artists steal; the best steal from the best; the great ones steal from those who can't sue. Go and ask Giuseppe Verdi.

Ask Verdi, still, however dead he is. He'll tell you; he'll set your right. Ask him about Otello. My man, Joey Green, Verdi made up convulsions and mess. When Verdi was finished, the only thing Otello had in common with Othello were the characters' names. Go on; ask him, ask him! Ask that other white man who screwed up Romeo and Juliet for his opera. On our stage, not even the writer is on our side. They are always on their own.

# THE LAST DAYS OR THE MEEK SHALL INHERIT THE EARTH

By Ardencie Hall-Karambe, PhD

*Playwright's Note: When we speak, we are conscious of an inner monologue—voice—that accompanies our spoken words. It is the same when I write. When writing, I call it the alternate; another version of the same idea yet told a different way. Most times, I ignore them. But this time I chose not to because they are important in establishing authenticity. They are echoes of my people's history in this country, and they ground me in the spirit connecting me to my praying fore parents. They are the foundation upon which the Main Voice is built; they are ever present. I call this is a fugue monologue for 3 voices. Voice 2 and Singer 3 should be prerecord and should be the same person who does Main Voice 1.*

**Main Voice 1:**
I'm tired... *(Singer 3 begins)*
I'm tired... *(Voice 2 begins)*
I'm tired
I'm tired of responding under duress.
I'm tired of being distressed
This place is about to blow up
And won't be no test
Get your fucking knee off my neck

The Last Days are drawing near
All of these people live in fear
It's very clear that
What we all feel is coming True
Like a second wave of the flu

(sneezing) hi-choo *(pre-recorded)*
God bless you
Just tested positive for Covid-19!
Who got a test?
Be Best

Dirt nap rest
Get your fucking knee off my neck

Everything has two or more truths
Yyyeeesss!
Depending on who you talking to
There was time when a picture spoke a thousand words
No more that's done
It has manifested
Run amuck
Splitting the time warp continuum
Causing all kinds of junk to get in there and get stuck
Stuck on me,
stuck on you, (singing) *"it's a feeling down deep in my soul that I just can't lose... yes, I'm on my way"*
See what I mean divergence is real!

Divergence is easy
Like a kitten chasing a light
Our videoed plight is highlighted
again and again
But it is not enough
It is split like an atom
Defused through a prism
"Oh the pretty lights!"
Must be a trick of the lens
Get your fucking knee off my neck.

This isn't new
Your knee has been resting there for
A century or two
And my oxygen is almost gone
And if I die before you wake.
Like others before me,
I promise it won't be in vain
For there are others feeling the pain.
The collective strain of communal sorrow

Runs deep in us and it is about exploded,
Unload all over you
Rushing lava and flying soot will cover everything
Destroying the old and making new land
Untarnished by your hands.

And my people will rise up
Throwing the mental and emotional shackles aside
As a new tide,
Rolls in,
A new day dawns.
Can't you feel a brand new day?

**Voice 2:**

*These lines are repeated throughout the piece fading out at the end as Main Voice 1 concludes.*

Blessed are the poor in spirit, for theirs is the kingdom of heaven.

Blessed are they who mourn, for they will be comforted.

Blessed are the meek, for they will inherit the land.

Blessed are they who hunger and thirst for righteousness, for they will be satisfied.

Blessed are the merciful, for they will be shown mercy.

Blessed are the clean of heart, for they will see God.

Blessed are the peacemakers, for they will be called children of God.

Blessed are they who are persecuted for the sake of righteousness, for theirs is the kingdom of heaven.

**Singer 3:**

*This is chain gang style song with the sounds of wood being pounded and steel clicking. Call and response style singing. Repeats until Main Voice 1 fades out.*

I'm gonna let my hammer ring

--hammer ring

I'm gonna let my hammer ring

--hammer ring

I'm gonna let my hammer ring

--hammer ring

Ring, ring, ring.

# DRAWING WHILE BLACK

By Maurice Moore

***Part 1: Drawing While Black***

White Eyes for sight/seeing/seen

White Ears for hearing/sound/vibrations

White Noses to Smell/Breath I can't breathe!

White Mouths/Wet/Spit/Dry/Buds Tongues to taste

White Skin/parts/limbs/flesh to Touch Feel/Felt.

What is Black sight?

Black sight is always having your worth measured by another's gaze.

(see. W.E.B. Dubois p. 2 - 3)

Black sight is not being represented from birth. Super Predator

Black sight means your presence casts no real lasting reflection in the world. Vampire

It's only when a self-imposed blindness occurs, I start to become visible; not just to the world, but to myself.

Aliveness of Line (UM Stamps mark 44:36 - 45:06)

Some White folks have all 5 human senses and some of us niggasfagsdarkies don't have any and/or possess full usage of these faculties. Regardless of what human senses niggas possess, the "Drawing While Black aka Black Boy Joy," performance is concerned with how a BlacktyBlackBlack art object in its various iterations and/or pro-cesses for someone of the African and African American Diasporas aka an art nigga like me are effected and affected by the -isms. By -isms, I mean anti-Black racism, mi-sogynoir, queer antagonism, Black Ablism ect… Moreover, how I code switch and mesh, cope, to navigate and do some of that magical Negro Bull shiting my way through this performance Snap!, and still continue to create this piece by tapping into Black aesthetics on my own terms. Witch

***Part 2: Drawing While Black:***

White Ears for hearing/sound/vibrations

What is Black sound? Hard (ers)

Black sound is That devil's music.

Black sound is strange fruit still growing. (see. Billie Holiday)

Black sounds are the police sirens.

Black sound is always worrying about making too much noise!

Black sound is the moan! Aunt Hester's Screams

(Moten p. 2 -3)

Ahaaw, I love to love you, baby.

(see. Donna Summer)

Pain Pleasure

Black sound is the silence when it comes to speaking the name of Nina Pop, another black trans woman murdered.

Black sound is the silence of how us Black Queers are constantly left out of hxstory.

Black sound is being a troublemaker!

Heavy Metal!

AfroPunk!

Funk!

Blues!

Country!

Classical!

Gospel! Getting Happy

BeBob! Made so y'all couldn't keep up, as if you could! Snap!

Rap!

When the music hits!

Hits my ears, it pours into my big black, blacklty, fat, body. (see. CB4)

Suddenly there are beats, rhythms, harmonies, and Pynk emanating from within.

No, Blues here, baby! I ain't Bessy either! But I ya Gurl! And, no my skin doesn't glisten beautiful shades of blue in de moonlight! Snap!

Only Negrx Faggtrey here boo! Yes, we on dat Zora TEA tonight!

(see. Jenkins)

(see. Janelle Monae) (see. Marlon T. Riggs p.390) (see. Zora)

I move my hips. My thick thighs feel feminine, vulgar, nasty, sticky, explicit, x rated...

I don't have rhythm! I can't dance! So, I must not be Black. Right? I am supposed to be able to dance! But sometimes I get in sync with the song(s)/lines, and I am like them, The other Black people. My ancestors are resurrected. I am resurrected. Zombie

I move like them. Maybe it's in my bad blood; the way I move my hips like the lines I create.

How do I know how to move like this, creating these types of lines?

Maybe, I am really Black instead of nothing. (see. Figure 2) Phantom Limbs

***Part 3: Drawing While Black***

Some White people's taste and smell don't have to be connected.

They are free to experience these sensations uninterrupted and without fear of death(s).

They/You have the freedom to do both at ease. necropolitics necromancy

black mouths/tongues for taste, black noses for smelling

Black taste and smell are connected.

For this performance, these scenes are about breathing.

Black breathing is holding your breath.

Black breathing is Drowning

Gasping

I can't breathe!

Like, de ancestor who flew back home. Dark Continent Flying Africans

(see. Diouf p.54)

Maybe they grew gills. Maybe dey found Atlantis? When performing the piece. I always make a mask of flowers. The flowers represent dat feminine energy, dat sissy shit, dat punk shit, dat quare shit. Yassss Queen!

I often forget to cut out nose holes so I can breathe. I keep this practice in when doing the performance. I like the sensation of not being able to breath. Death Wish

No, I like the sensation of having or feeling like I have some control over my own Black breathLife. Just as I take my White eyes away to gain Black sight. I have to take my White breath away to feel my Black breath. I can feel my breath for once, and for once it is all mine! Snap!

I am the Blackest in these moments. Breathing the same complicated air my ancestors did when they were are still bein chased,

In the Bowels of the ship,

Or Seasoned,

Made into Whipped Cream.

***Part 4: Drawing While Black***

White epidermis - used to feel/felt

White skin is the fair, the fairest of them all, snow, pure, clean, easy, smooth, light, goodness, genius, cis, beginning, healthy, alpha, wealth, academic, formal, privilege, civilized, invisible, centered, feather, visible, whatevah it wants to be, the default...

De complexion fo de protection.

(See. Paul Moony)

I mean, I could go on and on and on, and on, and on like Missy! Snap!

(See. Missy Elliot)

Black Skin/parts/limbs/flesh to Touch Feel/Felt

Black skin is weight. Cain

Marks

Cain Making Marks on paper. By the way, what's up with all dis white paper?

Making Cain marks on paper. Now, I can make cain marks in the air.

Cain punishment? "fugitive and wanderer"

Diaspora! Well If dat ain't a Nigga I don't know what one is! Snap!

Black isn't a fake tan Sweety!

Nah, you can't bottle dat shit up! Karen! Becky! Susan!, Tod!

Black skin isn't a fetish!

Black skin is?

What does my skin feel like? What does it feel like when moving through the world(s).

Drawing with Black skin feels/felt like weight.

Drawing with Black skin feel/felt like trouble.

I can see what havin this Black does when I am not doin dis performance. No, not just with my White eyes. With my Black feel/felt sense.

Black skin is noticing that I am the only one in the room. However, with this perfor-mance being the only one in the room it's on my terms! Snap!

Black skin is noticing in your eyes, how you won't sit next to me on the bus!

Black skin is always fitting the description.

Black skin was being a child, but being perceived as an adult.

Black skin is being seen as only a TOP! Or some funkin big dicked mandingo!

Bottom Pride Bitches!!!!!!

Black skin is feeling you clutch your tacky ass bags on the elevator.

Black skin is a feeling. The feeling is you punching me in the gut.

Black feel/felt is you crossing the street when you see/saw/feel/felt me comin.

Black feel/felt is finally moving through a space without feeling the touch of your White gaze for once! Snap!

## VOCABULARY

**Black Boy Joy** - is drawing with the Black senses, and this may be through feel-ing/tough i.e. one has to take away their White Gaze eyes, taste, smell, and breath in order to access drawing while black. And, through this manipulation of the senses a joy can be achieved that's rooted in Blackness that's situated in exploring both the ug-liness and beauty of existing while Black.

**Black Breath** - is purposefully hindering/restricting your breath; to take control over your life. To feel your breath/life on your own terms.

**Black CPT** - is this the immediacy. The feel/sensation of knowing your life could be taken from you at any moment just for being Black. And, still choosing to create/live.

**Black Feel/Felt** - is not just the sensation of touching your skin, but feeling/felting both the visible and invisible consequences of having Black skin.

**Black Sight** - is a forced blindness. The removal of the white gaze; to perceive both the beauty and the ugliness of Blackness on one's own terms.

**Black Sound** - is channeling/tapping into both the pleasure and pain of the moan.

**Drawing While Black** - Black drawings Language. Whether, I draw with lines that are corporal or in the air with lines that are non-corporal or archival, and now even as I draw with lines that are text.

# CERTAIN ASPECTS OF CONFLICT IN THE NEGRO FAMILY

## A Sonnet From A Negro To A Cop

By Tylie Shider

**CLIF:**

good morning officer/ good morning sir
i am headed easterly for breakfast
no sir i ain't got no weapon on me
gone. you can search my body and see:

*CLIF is searched.*

i understand trouble is in the street:
looters and shooters is what i am told
those kids are up to no good i agree
as for me, Sunday is reserved for peace

ain't got a list of grievances to air
a man ain't owed nothing but work and pay
"yessir in that order/ in that order"
"you know what it is/ you know what it is"

it is a game of follow the leader:
one kid picks up a brick and his friend joins

# I'M TIRED

By Rachel Lynett

**BECS:** This shit is exhausting.

*BECS moves center stage or downstage or away from the main "playing action." As she talks, GABRIELA, ISABEL, and PATRICK start to take pieces of the set apart and off-stage.*

*A strike happening during the show.*

It is exhausting writing plays about this shit. My name isn't Becs. My name is [name of the actor] but right now, I'm speaking to you as if I'm Rachel Lynett, the playwright.

I have written Good Bad People, Apologies to Lorraine Hansberry, Well-Intentioned White People, and Outrageous all about racism. All about how subtle micro-aggressions lead to black people being killed in the street. How many more plays do you need? I'm fucking tired.

Here's how this play was going to happen. The next day Becs goes to a protest and gets teargassed. And arrested. Jade has to bail her out. Becs and Isabel get into an argument about the best way to protest and Becs calls out Isabel for being a fake ally. Patrick catches the end of the fight and accuses Becs of being emotionally manipulative. Then, they're all back on the patio. BIG fight about intersectional politics and identities. The play ends with Jade having a major monologue about terms like people of color versus just saying black people and how black people and black churches have been on the front lines of EVERY OTHER FIGHT and yet we're fighting this one without help from fellow "POC." Becs and Patrick get into a major argument about race, wealth and privilege. It ends with Becs saying she's leaving. Patrick says "I'm telling the university about you dating a student." And the last line of the play would've been "That's how all of this violence starts. Just with a simple basic threat." Becs storms off stage. Lights down on Patrick and Gabriela and Isabel on the patio.

But you know what? Writing these plays is emotionally draining. Honestly. It's exhausting to sit at my computer and keep writing these fucking plays and then nothing happens. Nothing changes. And three days from now another black person has died for no other reason than being black.

And then the Black playwrights pull out their computers and go "here we fucking go again' and we ask Black actors to take on these roles that are just fucking heavy. And traumatic. And we're asking our own community to do a glorified minstrel show just so a couple of white people — that's you — can get a hard on from white guilt. But, oh wait.

It has to end happy. It has to end with hope. We have to believe that there's something better. Theatre is about challenging the people.

Is it?! One of the top Broadway producers is a major Trump supporter. (Hey Nederlander!) Theatre tickets are inaccessible, so audiences frequently are middle to upper class white people who usually get some sort of masochistic kick out of being told they're pieces of shit for 90 to 120 minutes.

I'm fucking tired. The emotional labor you're asking me to do is not worth the royalty check. The emotional labor you're making me to ask Black actors to do is too fucking heavy of an ask. I'm tired of explaining that white violence begins with little passive comments, little passive commentary. With silence. With knowing damn well not a single one of you would want to be a black person living in American today but also you're doing nothing about it to make life better for us.

It begins with loving Beyoncé and Lizzo and singing all the songs but then thinking that black people are less intelligent and lazy. By saying things like "black girl magic" but not actually listening to the black women that work in your offices. If there even are any.

Stop expecting us to carry your guilt and show you the way to be better. Stop expecting our art to be civility lessons and then punishing us for it by calling it "identity politics."

*At this point the stage should be bare. All the other characters are off stage.*

Fuck you for doing this to us. I won't write another play about this. I don't care how good it could be. I don't care if it's the play that could win a Tony. Stop forcing Black artists into corners where all we can write about is our pain. Let us tell our stories and accept that you have no place in it. And still show up for it. Still support it. I've supported many white stories in theatre. It's time for a fucking change.

I want to write about being Afro-Latinx, what it means to be both and neither at the same time. The blurred lines within my own identity. I want to write about my queerness. I want to write romantic comedies and plays that ask much harder questions than "Can you please stop killing black people?"

I'm fucking tired of writing plays about this. If you're tired of seeing them, then why aren't you doing anything about it?

LIGHTS UP ON THE AUDIENCE.

Be better.

# CREATE THE SPACE

By Cris Eli Blak

I don't really know what you want me to say. I mean, sometimes it feels like I need to yell as loud as I possibly can but then the very next day I feel like if I open my mouth a bullet might fly into it. Maybe that sounds crazy to you. Maybe it sounds like I'm overreacting. I've been told that a lot recently: "Not everything is political. Stop being so dramatic." Or, on the other end: "I'm so sorry about your loss," as if all of us are cousins or something. You know the one that gets me, though? It's when people tell me that they are so mad that these things have started happening. They tell me how tragic it is, how they can't believe these things happen this year. And it just confuses me because it happened last year too. And the year before that and the year before that and ten years before that and twenty years before that and one hundred years before that. So what's more tragic? The fact that these things keep on happening or that you're just now caring to notice it?

I'm getting ahead of myself. I'm an artist. I write. I tell stories. I'm supposed to create something in my mind, make it real then give it to the world. I don't feel like telling stories right now. I don't feel like giving my time, my work out to a world that doesn't care about me at all. What am I supposed to say? What words am I supposed to use? Do I cry? Do I fight? If I cry I'm not strong enough. If I fight I'm nothing but another angry black man with a chip on his shoulder. My white friends feel guilty. I'm getting sick and tired of them checking in on me, telling me that they "see" me. What does that mean? Was I invisible before?

I sit down and try to write something meaningful. Something real. I want to change the world but I know that I can't. I refuse to take the social media route and say that it's time for these things to end because, let's be honest, racism is not a disease that we can cure. That's the truth. I don't like it any more than you do but we have to face it. These things go so much deeper than here and now. I don't want the whole world to love and respect me. It isn't possible! I just want to feel safe when I walk outside my door. I want to be able to take a second to take a breath.

But how can I ever take a breath again when "I can't breathe" is all anyone who looks like me can say? This has to be a nightmare. Go ahead and change something. Change everything! Try. You can change laws. You can change statues. But you can't change someone's heart. You can't change the names they call me when I'm in a neighborhood that some people feel I don't belong. You can't change the history of my family — our families. There is no greater pandemic than that of men and women who look like me being murdered in cold blood on the streets of cities throughout the country, throughout the world. There's no way to say all of their names. We don't have enough time in a day.

Writer. Right. My job is to create a space and fill it with words. Every task comes with the question of what words will I decide to fill this space with? I sit down again after, who knows, probably hours of pacing around my room, chewing my nails to the skin, trying to think of the right words to say in a world where I am too often silenced. Then I get it. I really get it. There is no right thing to say. Nothing is right anymore. It hasn't been for the longest time. I just have to say something, because my voice is the strongest weapon I got right now. My heartbeat, so long as I got one, can be used as the backing track to the most beautiful brown-skinned song you've ever heard. There's no time to waste, there's no point in chasing clout when half the people we're supposed to trust have no idea what they're talking about.

I'm gonna write about love. I'm gonna write about hate because you cannot have one without the other. You cannot ignore it. If you do it will show its ugly face to you sooner than you'd like.

It's time for us to create a space. A space of our own. A space for our praise and a space for our pain. A place for our cries when another kid dies. A space like this. Just like this. A space where I can open my heart and let the words fall out like pieces from a game board.

And I need to put it down on the page quick. Let's face it, none of us know when our voices will be taken away.

# MOTHER TO SON

By Crystal D. Mayo

Black Lives Matter..... is not a catchy hook of a hip hop banger. It's not a gimmick or fad. Those words are more than stenciled letters on a black t -shirt. They're phonemes that hold memory, antiguos energy from the middle passage. From black bodies stacked on top of one another with shackled ankles in crowded rows. From African mothers surrendering their infants to the obsidian waves of the ocean. From slave women whose mistresses steal their natural maternal instincts, forcing them to become wet nurses to their white babies. Foreign lips suckle their breasts while their own suffer. Brown bellies swelled from hunger that dirty water and sour cow's milk cannot sustain.

Black Lives Matter were the three words that guided Arminta's footsteps through the woods following the drinking gourd to lead over 300 slaves to freedom. It's in the hundreds of enslaved bodies that toiled to build the rooms of the White House but until 1868 were denied the right to vote. It's the calluses of black hands that labored in swamp lands hammering nails into steel tracks only to be sequestered to the "Colored Section." A Green book nestled under their arms on the same track their labor built. It's... in the raspy undertone of Lady Day singing the blues, southern trees bearing a strange fruit. Blood on the leaves. Blood on the root.

If Black Lives Mattered there wouldn't have been Jim Crow laws with false claims of lives that would be separate and equal, its colored and white signs oversee everyday life of segregation..... humiliation. Back doors to movie theaters, ten seats behind white passengers on buses and sketches of bare feet on brown paper bags.

"Black Lives Matter" whispered the spirit of the ancestors who locked the bodies of Claudette Colvin and Rosa Parks in their seats on a public bus, echoed in the trodden footsteps of the bus boycott and sat in defiance of the "Whites Only" sign with four Greensboro college men at the Woolworth lunch counter.

It was the silent prayer of thousands of men and women who on bended knee bowed their heads before bully clubs, sharp tooth dogs and tear gas cultivating God's day into a bloody one. And in 1954 Brown vs Board of Topeka, Thurgood Marshall argued the psychological damage of segregation, the systematic inequality that promotes inferiority and a school system inherently unequal, proved to the world that black lives did matter. Its value, its importance, vibrated from the treetops of Washington DC. Echoed in the sea of black, brown and white faces united in the vision of the Promise land.

If all lives matter why is the study of black history shortened to 28 days of a year and taught as an elective? Why do American history books teach children that the evolution of black life began shackled in slavery when the roots of our beginnings are the birthplace of algebra, geometry and calculus before the roots of our identity, our language, and our culture were sold on auction blocks. If black lives did matter why are our contributions negated, our music prefabricated without respect for its sole proprietor. Ours stories written by pseudo authors, told through foreign tongue and lens. Who can truly understand our own resilience but we? The devalue of our lives is institutionalized and its residuals silently passed down in our children's DNA. And we can't get over it. But we do relive it from one generation to the next. From Emmett Till, to Trayvon Martin, from the Tulsa Massacre, to the streets of Minneapolis Minnesota. The ancestral cycle repeats itself over and over again until... we watch right in front of our eyes like the generations before us just how black lives in America don't matter. As a knee obstructs an airway for eight minutes and 46 seconds. Until a grown man cries out for his deceased mother. Until a body grows limp and the internal patches of our ancestral quilts holding our generational trauma weep for a man most of us never knew but understand that he is our husband. He is our son. He is our brother.

He is me................

Black Lives Matter.... from Africa.... to auction blocks.... To Juneteenth... to Jim Crow.... to desegregation, to integration to 2020.

We.... have always mattered. We are the fabric of American life........ we are the inspiration behind The words of Langston Hughes...

I too........ am America.

# HAPPY BIRTHDAY

By Dr. Mary E. Weems

*Setting: City street. Park bench sits downstage center. JAQUISHA enters dressed in white silk blouse, red leather skirt, and red pumps. She's smoking an electric cigarette. She's carrying a large Black purse slung over one shoulder. She sits down, balances the electric cigarette on the edge of the bench. She takes a journal and pen out of her purse, holds it to her a chest for a few moments, as if waiting for words to come.*

**JAQUISHA:** (begins writing and talking out loud) Dear Ex-Police Officer:

I've been a Christian all my life. Not the kind that goes to church every Sunday, then forgets the pastor's words and everything they've ever studied in the bible the moment they walk outside, or the kind that attends a church where everybody but the pastor's wife knows he not only has a woman who sits in the same pew as his wife, then sneaks into his office after hours to give him something under his desk, he doesn't talk about in the pulpit. (beat) What I mean is, I was raised by a mother who believed that we are all God's children with all her heart, who even though she grew up in the South in the 1940s and 50s believed that everybody was equal, even the white folks she saw hate her enough to push her off the sidewalk when she forgot her place when they were walking by. Mr. Man, my mother may have been the only person in my neighborhood who just refused to hate white folks. Fact, during a time when Blacks were getting lynched on a regular basis, she started dinner and talking meetings at her house on a monthly basis. She'd hand write invitations to 7 Black people and 7 White folks each time, cook a bunch of good food, shape her living room into a circle of chairs and wait. Whoever came, got a good meal, followed by an hour or two of talking about the issues of the day, personal stuff and plans of action. (beat) We moved up North in 1960, she met her husband who became my father and here I am today. (beat) I share all this because, now that I know you're in jail till Never, that I'll never have to see you again in this or the next life since we're going to two different places, I want you to know a little about the woman you raped (Pause) like I was a blow up doll you bought and paid for in places people go looking for a substitute for love. (beat) Before you violated my temple, this body created like yours in God's image, I'd only had sex with two men in my life. Johnny Watson, when I was 17 and he was 18 and then only after we'd kissed and hugged and fooled around for weeks. He gave me a cigar band engagement ring, told me he loved me and asked me to marry him once I turned 18. (beat) Unfortunately, God had another plan for him cause he enlisted in the army right after he graduated and died in Viet Nam after stepping on a land mind, right before my birthday. (beat) I was 22 before I dated again. Took mother's advice and went away to school right after I graduated, became a school teacher. That day you stopped me for swerving on the street, when I wasn't, I was on my way home after working with three of my 5th graders on their homework. Funny. Even though I got that weak feeling in my gut that means trouble's coming, I just thought you were going to give me a ticket I didn't deserve. Had no idea you were about to take something from me it's still hard to talk about to the only other man I've given my body to, my husband of 25 years. (beat) I tell everybody I don't remember, that I was too afraid you were going to kill me, but as God is my witness, I lie every time I say it. (beat) Funny. I hate liars and try my best to always tell the truth, but I finally found something I just can't say out loud. (beat) That day, when I took out my license and registration, you looked at me dead in my eye, told me "Get the fuck out of this car bitch and into my cruiser," held my arm soon as I stood up afraid to even look around to see if anybody was watching, locked me in your car which has "Protect and Serve" painted on the side and took me to an alley. (beat) You got me on my knees, put your privates in my face, told me to open my mouth and banged my head against a slimy brick wall until you got tired. Then you pushed me down, jerked up my skirt, snatched down my white panties and raped me until you screamed your own name out loud (beat). My spirit went into survival mode. I laid still as the dead until you caught your raggedy breath. Followed your instructions to pull myself together, except my panties which you kept, and get back in your car. Then you just took me back to where my car was illegally parked, tore up the ticket one of your fellow officers had left on it and told me if I told anybody what happened to me, you know where I live. (beat) Well, as you know by now, you picked the wrong Black woman that day. Wasn't until I'd told my husband and had him go with me after I called the po-lice to file charges against you and these other 12 sisters came forward that I found out you was preying on us like a white wolf who thinks every time he gets hungry he supposed to eat whatever he wants. Staying on the poor, Black side of town, targeting Black women in trouble with the law, using drugs, selling themselves. (beat) You actually believe that we're worthless, that none of us would come forward and if we did, nobody would believe us. (beat) Funny. None of us can believe how wrong you were about that, how an all-white jury could not only find you guilty as hell, but recommend over 250 years in the penitentiary. TWO HUNDRED and FIFTY years. And the best part of all, the icing on the cake I made soon as I got home that day after the verdict, was you got the news on your 29th birthday.

*She closes her journal, puts it and her pen back in her purse, picks up her electric cigarette with a big smile and takes a puff before she exits stage right.*

# KNOCK

By Rajendra Ramoon Maharaj
( Excerpt from *The Mis-Education of America*)

*In a pool of light, BLACK stands in front of the Barclays Center in Downtown Brooklyn at a Black Lives Matter, peaceful, non-violent rally holding a bullhorn. Black is wearing a NAACP t-shirt and baseball cap. They are sweating profusely standing on an apple box surrounded by members of the NAACP Brooklyn Branch, Color of Change, and the Black Lives Matter Movement.*

*Into the bullhorn.*

**BLACK:** Knock! Knock! Knock! Knock!
Knock! Knock! Knock!
Knock! Knock!
Knock!
Knock!
Knock!

*BLACK puts the bullhorn down.*

Our story... my story... this story begins with a hemlock growing out of the very soul of America. America, you are changing right in front of my very own eyes each second of the three hundred and sixty-five days.

*Into the bullhorn.*

Knock!
Knock!
Knock!

Let me in!... Let us in!... Is anyone home?... No one is home?... What is home?... No one fucking cares... No one hears, and for me... for us... for me... there may be no tomorrow... No today... No tomorrow. Please, open up! Let me in!... Let us in!.. Can you hear me?!... Can you see me?!... Does my fucking story matter?! Is anyone in there?!

*Puts the bullhorn down.*

I think I see you trembling in a corner losing your religion in the deep dark lies and fears that keep you warm like a blanket late at night. But that's not real! That's not fucking reality! I've been waiting so long to be let in!... We've been waiting so long to be let in. Please... Is anyone in there?... Hello?...

*Into the bullhorn.*

Knock!
Knock!
Knock!

Motherfuckers, Wake up!... Wake up!... Wake the fuck up, America!!

*Puts the bullhorn down.*

Brooklyn, I'm thinking about our brother George Floyd, y'all. About the shrieks, and the ears they pierced— those standing by in horror and trying to intervene, being pushed back, filming it to bear witness, to attest to it later— and the ears— and knees and arms and hands—of those who would not hear, who would burden and crush him, who, could not be moved, who had to be forcefully removed even after his murder.

*Into the bullhorn.*

I can't breathe!
Do not kill me!
Mama!
7 minutes 46 seconds?
Mama!
8 minutes 46 seconds?
Mama!
9 minutes 30 seconds?

*Puts the bullhorn down.*

Brooklyn, the hardest thing in the world is to love someone who doesn't love you back. The anguish of an unrequited love. But what do you do when that love is for a country that doesn't care about you, or think about you until the next election cycle?

*Into the bullhorn.*

Knock!
Knock!
Knock!

*Puts the bullhorn down.*

Yo, Brooklyn, since the murders of Ahmaud Arbery Breonna Taylor and George Floyd, I think of my own mortality every day in America... do you? How my mortality is tied to my own American dreams realized and my dreams that are deferred. The thing is, you can have the greatest paint in the world, but does it really matter if you don't have a canvas to paint on?

The quintessential American Dream may still be out of my grasp, just like it was for my grandpa and his grandpa and his grandpa. When I was a kid sitting on my stoop, on grandpa's knee, I thought the American Dream was the same for everybody, I really did. White picket fence, dog, spouse, a couple of kids. All of the nation is at peace; we have a military but no war. I make enough money to go on vacation once a year doing something I love.

Because of this moment and this movement with y'all, I have a different American dream now. I want to live in the pursuit of pleasure. I want to live freely and openly and happily surrounded by art and love and people who are also in pursuit of their own pleasures. I want to be a part of a family that can be who they are and walk through this world courageously and unafraid.

A nation where there are no poor black folks in jail for a nickel-bag! While rich white millennials in Hollister tie-die t-shirts, Vans, and skinny jeans can open up shops and boost their white ass small town economies through cannabis products! Y'all feel me?! My American dream is living in this fucking country the way I want to live and not apologizing for a goddamn thing!

My American dream means if I get slaughtered in the street and millions of people watch, my murderer goes to jail. My dream is the police and their gun toting sympathizers seeing the repercussions of said conviction and thinking twice before killing our brother, George, in the street or our sister, Breonna, in her bed... in her fucking bed, y'all! Those motherfuckers murdered our sister,

Breonna, in her bed!

*Into the bullhorn.*

BK, say her name!
Breonna Taylor!
Breonna Taylor!
Breonna Taylor!

*Puts the bullhorn down.*

Back in the day when I was a kid growing up on the block in Bed-Stuy I asked my mama if she had to go to the bodega and she looked me in the face, stared long and hard into my deep, dark brown eyes, and with her beautiful honeybee stung lips, she smiled at me and said...

(in mama's voice) "Baby, the only thing mama gotta' do is stay black and die..." I guess mama was right... I guess that sums it up, Brooklyn... Our American Dream... Stay black and die... That's the dream... (whispers) Stay black and die... Black and die... Black and die... and die...

*Into the bullhorn.*

Knock!
Knock!
Knock!

*Puts the bullhorn down.*

America... I'm begging you... We're begging you... Let us in... Let me in... Is anyone there?...

*Into the bullhorn.*

Motherfuckers, Wake up!... Wake up!... Wake the fuck up, America!!

Knock! Knock!    Knock! Knock!
Knock! Knock! Knock!
Knock! Knock!
Knock!
Knock!
Knock!

*Loud police sirens are heard. BLACK slams the bullhorn to the ground. Several gunshots ring out.*

BLACKOUT

# APPENDEX A — BIOS

**Nessa Amherst** is an actress and writer who has three simple rules for the words she puts to paper: be honest, be transparent, and be kind. Originally from Chicago, she has worked with companies and organizations from within and outside the DC/MD/VA area. Some of her favorite performances include *Lotto & Raffles & Sweepstakes, Oh My!* (PlayZoomers), *As You Like It* (TheatreLab DC), *The Wednesday Train* (The Organic Theatre), *Medea* (Globe Online), *Runtime Error* (Transformation Theatre), *Two Gentlemen of Verona* (JaYo Théâtre), and *These Violent Delights* (Letter of Marque Theater Co.) Define "Black" was one of many original monologues featured in the online performance *Monologues of the Black Experience*, directed by Jacqueline Elisabeth. You can check out more of her writings and career at nessaamherst.com.

**********

Passionate playwright, author, and assistant professor, **Melda Beaty** resides in Chicago, Illinois with her three gifted and beautiful daughters. Melda has penned five plays with national productions in Houston, Atlanta, Pittsburgh, Winston-Salem, etc. Presently and happily, she is a 2021 Confluence Fellow with the St. Louis Shakespeare Festival. In addition, she is a freelance contributor to Black Masks Magazine. Before playwriting, she wrote two books: My Soul to His Spirit: Soulful Expressions from Black Daughters to Their Fathers and Lime. Melda earned her B.A. in Broadcast Communications at the University of Illinois at Urbana-Champaign and her M.A. in English at Illinois State University. The goal and vision of her art is to bring the narratives of marginalized "grown folks" to the stage in a way that honors black experiences and reflect the humanity in black life. https://meldacreates.com/

**********

**Jonathon "Jack-Jack" Benjamin** is a proud veteran of the U.S. Air Force. He graduated from the George Washington University in May 2018, Magna Cum Laude, with a major in Theatre and a minor in Creative Writing, concentrating on Playwriting. He was raised on Fort Lewis, Washington and enlisted in the military not long after high school. In 2013, he sustained serious injuries while on active duty. After spending two years in hospital care, Jack-Jack was medically retired from the Air Force in 2015. In that same year, he enrolled at the George Washington University. Then, as a Senior, his first play, "American Airman," was awarded the Clayssen's Award for Undergraduate playwriting. The play was further honored as a semi-finalist at the Kennedy Center's American College Theatre Festival in January 2018. Jonathon's full-length, one-act and 10-minute plays, as well as his monologues, can be found on the New Play Exchange. In his words, "Playwriting gave me a sense of agency over my experiences and created an unapologetic playwright from the fiery furnace of life's volatility." His work's aim is to bring an audience to the same euphoria that he has found in playwriting. "Theatre is a miracle of the human experience and so, I must write. Not because I can, but because it is how I live."

**********

**Mardee Bennett** is a playwright and actor. He is a 2021 National Black Theatre (Harlem, NY) Playwrights Residency Finalist. His new play CANE is a 2021 Blue Ink Finalist and Bonnie & Terry Burman New Play Award Semi-Finalist (Barrington Stage).

His play THE REAPERS ON WOODBROOK AVENUE was a Eugene O'Neill Playwrights Conference Finalist, Seven Devils Playwrights Conference Finalist, Princess Grace Award Semi-Finalist and Bonnie & Terry Burman New Play Award Semi-Finalist.

His plays have been developed with Center Stage, Signature Theatre, National Black Theatre, Quarantine Reading Society and Baltimore Playwrights Festival. Other Plays: In the Ramble; Loretta; The Nerve; A Pleasant Place To Be. Mardee trained at New York University's Tisch School of the Arts.

He is represented by A3 Artists Agency.

**********

**Cris Eli Blak** is an award winning and internationally produced writer for the page, stage and screen. His work has garnered him a Bronze Remi from the Worldfest Houston International Film and Video Festival, the Christopher Hewitt Award in Fiction, a Pushcart Prize nomination and honors from Vectis Radio, Negro Ensemble

Company, Clocktower Players and A is For. His work has been produced, performed and/or published around the world, from Off-Broadway (Urban Stages and Rattlestick Playwrights Theatre), West Coast (Theatre of NOTE, Theatre West, Common Ground Theatre, Left Edge Theatre and Breath of Fire Latina Theater Ensemble), Collegiate (Columbia University, York College, Academy of Arts University and Wellesley College), London (The Quean's Theatre and Flawstate), Australia (Melting Pot Theatre), and Ireland (Eva's Echo). He is developing new work with Derby City Playwrights, The Road Theatre, Imaginarium Theatre Company and Et Alia Theater. He continues to strive to create work that reflects the world that we live in, with all of its different and diverse colors, creeds and cultures.

**********

**Sharnell Blevins** has a BA in Business and an MFA in Creative Writing from Mount Saint Mary's University. Her play, "Dreams on a Dime" is from her MFA thesis, "Lottery Winner." In 2020, "Dreams on a Dime" was a semi-finalist in the SheLA/SheNYC Play Festival and read at the San Diego Repertory's Kuumba Fest; her story "COVID Prisms was read during The Billie Holiday Theatre's Love in the Time of Corona, 50in50. Sharnell's poems, "Ruling" and "preparations" were published in IO Literary Journal inaugural edition. Her blog, 'Thank God It's Friday" was published on Elev8.com.

Sharnell is a member of Women Who Submits Editorial Team for its 2021 anthology; and was an Editor of The Rush Literary Journal. She is a member of the Association of Writing Professionals and Programs, Dramatist Guild, Kite City Playwrights, New Play Exchange, Playwright's Center, and Women Who Submit. Sharnell Blevins lives in the Los Angeles area with her husband, Clifton, and their six children. sharnellblevins.com

**********

**Sharon Cleveland Blount** has emerged as a LA playwright. She received her MFA in Creative Writing, from Mount Saint Mary's University in Los Angeles. "Unexpectedly, I re-discovered a passion for writing plays. I was transported back to elementary school days where I remembered the joys of playwriting. Once you have a finished script, you can bring your vision, your words, right to the stage. That is empowering." Her play, Weave Addiction, was workshopped in the Fall of 2019, at Hollywood's Sunset Gower Studios.

When life came to a halt in 2020, Sharon honed in on her monologue writing skills. Not Made To Be Your Maid, was featured in 50in50: Letters to Our Sons, a collection of monologues, performed at The WACO Theater in North Hollywood, California, March 7-8, 2020. The production carried over and was also performed on Facebook Live through Brooklyn's Billie Holiday Theater in April, 2020.

"Telling my own, and sharing other peoples' stories, is my passion." It is what inspired--HerShe Productions—a vehicle for visionaries and creatives to share their voices, experiences and telling of their stories in the most alluring genre and format for maximum audience reception. "Everyone has a story--most people want their story heard."

**********

**Christopher Buchanan** is a New York City based playwright, performer and producer. His play Ad Nauseam was produced as a world premiere in the Blurring Boundaries short play festival by The New Ambassadors Theatre Company. Angels Watching From Afar and The Rule Book Can't Apply both received readings by The PlayGround Experiment with the latter being featured in a second reading by The Polar Bear Theatre Company. As a performer, Christopher was the title character in Mr. Long for the Frigid New York Festival. In his hometown of Washington, DC, he appeared as Klingon Hamlet in Avant Bard Theatre's By Any Other Name: An Evening of Shakespeare in Klingon, featuring George Takei and Stephen Fry. He portrayed famed scientist Raymond Gosling in the world premiere of Photograph 51 for Active Cultures Theatre. Christopher also appeared in productions for Rorschach Theatre, Theatre Lab of Washington, Unstrung Harpist and Lazy Susan Dinner Theatre. Christopher studied playwriting in New York City at Primary Stages' Einhorn School of Performing Arts and acting in Washington, DC at the Theatre Lab Academy of Dramatic Arts and the Studio Theatre Acting Conservatory.

**********

**Cashel Campbell** makes her public debut as a 08:46 selected author. She has always been an avid writer - with journals, poems & essays that date back to her early childhood.

A native New Yorker, Cashel began her artistic endeavors successfully as a child actor (SAG-AFTRA est.1987). Alongside her pursuits, she has become a dancer, performance artist (theatre & dance expression) and in 2016 achieved a Masters of Science in the Creative Arts Therapy field as a Dance/Movement Psychotherapist from Pratt Institute.

In 2018, Cashel created Feel Heal Dance, a dance/movement psychotherapy & spiritual counseling practice that integrates holistic approaches such as: talk therapy, advanced Reiki, intuitive counseling & Soulography- a pole dance as therapy intervention. Leading with joy and an empathetic heart, Cashel offers clients the opportunity to build social, emotional & communication skills through creativity, compassion & movement. An often keynote speaker & guest lecturer, she is devoted to carving out a space for authenticity within the emotional healing & self evolvement movement.

About the piece: Cashel wrote #HashTagTheBlackGirl in 2016. It is written as an open letter to the author's self and the society she resides in. It's the author's reflective reality & her attempt to accept the vulnerability & the pain of living projected upon, racially stereotyped, objectified & rejected in her "home" country of America.

**********

**Max King Cap** is a visual artist from Chicago who now lives in Los Angeles. His work has been seen in galleries and museums in Vienna, New York, Stuttgart and numerous other cities in Europe and the US. In addition to receiving visual art awards from the Artadia and Creative Capital foundations he is also a writer whose work has appeared in The Racial Imaginary, Threepenny Review, Shenandoah, The Puritan, and TriQuarterly. His play, The Drop, a drama that pairs the life of Ota Benga and the Klondike Gold Rush, is currently in preproduction. He earned his MFA from the University of Chicago, his doctorate from USC, and has taught at

Columbia College Chicago, Illinois Institute of Technology, and Pitzer College.

**********

**Shaneisha Dodson** is an entrepreneur, a public speaker and the founder of Black Girlz Productions. She writes, directs and produces plays. Her productions have toured across the United States. Dodson has won numerous awards for her work as an entrepreneur: 2019 Best Artist,Top 35 Women in Business, Women Doing It Big Honoree, Top 40 under 40, Best Playwright and 2017 Best Theatrical Presentation winner to name a few. In her spare time, she enjoys writing, dancing and spending time with loved ones.

**********

**Vincent Terrell Durham** is an award winning playwright who hails from Binghamton, New York. He strives to create thought-provoking, character driven narratives. He writes to pay honor to the Johnson family, the best storytellers a little Black boy could ever have.

**********

**Zachariah Ezer** is an M.F.A. Playwriting Candidate at the University of Texas at Austin. He is a James A. Michener Fellow for the class of 2023, a 2020 Town Stages Sokoloff Creative Arts Fellow, a 2018 BUFU EYEDREAM Resident, a 2015 Wesleyan University Olin Fellow, and a member of The Tank's LIT Council. He is also a dramaturg (for The National Black Theatre, foolsFURY, and The Workshop Theater, where he is currently in residence), an essayist (published by Gizmodo/io9, HuffPost, and elsewhere), and a performer (in alternative rock band Harper's Landing). His work animates theoretical quandaries through dramaturgical forms, and his artistic project is the development of an Afropessimist aesthetics, in order to find a way to represent the narrative arc of the slave.

**********

**Tina Fakhrid-Deen** is a writer and professor whose writing and research interests include Afrocentricity, hood feminism, hip-hop culture, and urban education. She is the author of Let's Get This

Straight: The Ultimate Handbook for Youth with LGBTQ Parents (Seal Press). Her play, Powerless Gods was a semi-finalist for the Bay Area Playwriting Festival (2019) and O'Neill Playwriting Conference (2016/2018). Tina's second play, Dandelions, was commissioned for Theatre on the Lake - In the Works, and received a developmental podcast play production as part of their 2020 season. Her third play, Pulled Punches, was developed through the Women's Theatre Alliance of Chicago and MPAACT in 2019 and the world premiere of Pulled Punches was slated for April 2020 with MPAACT at the Greenhouse Theater, but has been postponed due to COVID. Tina is a 2020 MacDowell Fellow, 2018 Kimbilio Fellow, and VONA Fellow in Fiction and Playwriting (2011/2017). Her public writing and cultural commentary have been featured in diverse media outlets and publications including The Root, NPR: Eight-Forty-Eight, News One, The Dr. Laura Berman Show on Oprah Radio, Not-for-Tourists, Jet, Pearson Scott Foresman, and several anthologies. Tina is a company member with MPAACT and can be reached at www.shespeaksrivers.com.

**********

**Leland Gantt** (playwright/project curator) is a writer and performer of RHAPSODY IN BLACK, an autobiographical solo show developed at The Actors Studio with Estelle Parsons as Directorial Consultant. LeLand self-produced RHAPSODY at the United Solo Festival in 2014, earning a "Best Storyteller" award for himself and a "Best Director" award for Estelle. Since then, LeLand has been touring RHAPSODY both nationally and internationally using it's "Prismatic reflections on blackness" to ignite and expand conversations about race and identity. A veteran of the stage, Mr. Gantt highlights playing both Iago and Othello, creating the roles of Benny the Jet in Keith Glovers's IN WALKS ED, and Tempest Landry in Walter Mosley's THE FALL OF HEAVEN (both world premiers at Cincinnati Playhouse in the Park) and most recently, playing Pontius Pilot in Stephen Adly Guirgus' LAST DAYS OF JUDAS ISCARIOT at La Mama, ETC. Other regional credits include: TWO TRAINS RUNNING and RADIO GOLF (Syracuse Stage); GEM OF THE OCEAN (Arena Stage), JITNEY and SEVEN GUITARS (Pittsburgh Public Theater), and IN WALKS ED (Longwharf Theater). Off-Broadway/Broadway: RHAPSODY IN BLACK (The WorkShop Theater), SLIPPERY WHEN WET (La Mama), ANOTHER MAN'S POISON (Peter Jay Sharpe

Theater), Marion McClinton's POLICE BOYS (Playwright's Horizons); Oyamo's KILLA DILLA and LET ME LIVE (Drama Desk and Audelco award nominee - Featured Actor), and the revival of MA RAINEY'S BLACK BOTTOM starring Whoopi Goldberg (u/s Rock Dutton). Film and Television credits include: Miracle at St. Anna, Requiem for a Dream, Malcolm X, Presumed Innocent, The Good Fight, Law and Order, Law and Order SVU, JAG and HBO's The Affair.

**********

**Michael Hagins** is an African-American Playwright, Director, Fight Director, Actor, and Producer. Michael is a Member of Dramatists Guild and an Advanced Actor-Combatant for the Society of American Fight Directors. Michael was born in Brooklyn, New York, but raised in a small town in Florida for his childhood. He has used the racism and prejudice he dealt with at an early age to fuel his writing, which he has done so since the age of 9. Michael is an avid lover of Shakespeare (he has done every play in the Shakespeare Canon) and has performed, directed and taken part in over 1,000 plays and films over his artistic career.

Off-Broadway: The Long Rail North (Soho Rep, FringeNYC). New York Productions: Basement (Roly Poly Productions); Michael is Black (Planet Connections Theatre Festivity); The Renaissance Dueling Plays (Planet Connections Theatre Festivity); The Vengeance Room (FRIGID Festival). Regional/Other: Hit and Match (Chicago Fringe, Johannesburg Fringe). Outstanding Playwriting - Hit and Match, 2013; Outstanding Overall Production of a Solo Show - Michael is Black. Artistic Director, C.A.G.E. Theatre Company

**********

**Ardencie Hall-Karambe, Ph.D.** is an associate professor of English/Theatre Arts at the Community College of Philadelphia. Ardencie co-founded and leads Arden Blair Enterprises, LLC (ABE), a multi-divisional enterprises that includes the semi-professional theatre company, Kaleidoscope Cultural Arts Collective (KCAC). She works as an educator, workshop facilitator, actress, director, playwright, composer, and designer. A brief history of Ardencie's work includes, performance: The Public Theatre, Theatre for The New City (TNC), P.S. 122 and other theatre in NYC; playwriting, composing, and directing: "Ain't Nobody...A Civil Right Musical,"

(2011, KCAC, NYC), "Lysistrata, Cross Your Legs Sister" (2019, KCAC, Barrymore Awards Recommended, PHILA), "#ALLLIVESDONTMATTER" (2020, KCAC, PHILA), "The Art of I AM," (2016, co-produced by KCAC, NYC); publishing: poetry "Sweet Daddy" in Philly Jawns: For Women Revisited, an anthology in tribute to Nina Simone (2021), The Actor's Tool Kit (2015), Not Your Grandmother's Table (2016); and television: co-produces, writes, and hosts "The Market,"(awarded an International Telly Award, and two Communicator's Broadcasting Awards in the areas of Educational and Social Awareness Programming, premiering 2014, CCPTV, PHILA), "Aunt Nancy's Stories" and "Black History Moments" (premiering 2021, CCPTV, PHILA).

**********

**Siri Imani** is quickly emerging as one of the Midwest's foremost young, black voices. Her poetry and music are infused with hard truths, tough love and visions of a better tomorrow.

Never has an artist been more open and honest on the stage than Siri Imani. She weaves together song and poetry to tell powerful stories of love and liberation; state and personal violence; social, environmental, racial and sexual justice; woman's empowerment and human transcendence.

Siri Imani is a boundary-breaking soul sister who has sharpened her art as a tool for popular education, community organizing and personal transcendence. She is a warrior woman writer not afraid to tell her personal truths while making biting social commentary on the world we live in.

**********

**James J. Johnson** is a professional actor (and as of late, playwright and screenwriter) with experience in stage, film, television and voice-overs. He currently resides in the DC Metro Area with his wife. He has appeared with many theatres across the area, including the African-Continuum Theatre Co., Arena Stage, Woolly Mammoth Theatre, Ford's Theatre, Theater J, Rep Stage, Kennedy Center, 1st Stage and Imagination Stage. He recently received a Solo Works commission from 1st Stage in Tyson's Corner, VA. He narrates audiobooks for Potomac Talking Books. As a voice actor, his voice appears in the new podcast "Seizing Freedom" and in various graphic novel audiobooks produced by Graphic Audio. J. J., as he is known to family and friends, is a proud member of both SAG-AFTRA and Actors' Equity Association. He received his B.F.A. from Virginia Commonwealth University in 1997, graduating magna cum laude. J. J. has taught "Intro to Acting" for DC's Theatre Lab since November 2020. He also works as an artist educator with BodyWise Dance, where he gets to collaborate with artists with special needs. A fervent believer in networking, J. J. is a co-founder of Galvanize DC, a local support network for Black theatre artists.

**********

**Louis Johnson** is the lead writer/co-creator of the web-series, "The Thrill of the Kill"@ likemindscreative.com. "T.O.T.K" was an official selection of Phoenix Comicon Film Festival 2017 in Phoenix, Az., May 25-28, 2017. In February '18, he was selected to be a Fellow at the Tennessee Playwright's Studio in Nashville, Tn. In November '18, his play "NEC Compuncti: (No Remorse)" had a staged reading in the Tennessee Playwright's Studio's Fall Festival of Plays at the Darkhorse Theatre in Nashville, Tn. In May/June '19, he directed his one-act play, "A Bullet for Jenny King" in ACT ONE Theatre Company's One Act Wednesdays at the Darkhorse Theatre in Nashville, Tn. In January '20, his play, "Makin' Bond" will have a staged reading in The Fade-to-Black Reading Series in Houston, Tx. In January '20, his play, "Makin' Bond" will be produced in The Secret Theatre Company's One-Act Play Festival in Long Island City, NY. In February '20, he directed his play, "Oh, the LIES we've told" In Act One Theatre Company's One-Act Play Festival at the Darkhorse Theatre in Nashville, Tn. Louis was a 2020 Finalist for the 2020-2021 Maison Baldwin Writer-in-Residence Award presented by Les Amis de la Maison Baldwin.

**********

**Rachel Lynett** (she/they) is a Black/Afro-Latine playwright and producer.. So far in 2021, her plays have been featured at Theatre Lab, Magic Theatre, True Colors, Florida Studio Theatre, Transformation Theatre, Edgewood College, and as part of the Amplified Series at Indiana University, Bloomington. Rachel Lynett is the 2021 recipient of the Yale Drama Prize for their play, *Apologies to Lorraine Hansberry (You Too August Wilson)* and their plays *Last Night* and *HE DID IT* made the 2020 Kilroy's List. Rachel

Lynett is also the Artistic Director of Rachel Lynett Theatre Company and Executive Director of Page by Page.

**********

**Antonio David Lyons**' artistic universe straddles the globe with one foot planted firmly in both South Africa and the USA. His creative spirit enjoys the balance of performing in front of the camera and nurturing meaningful projects through the production process.

Lyons holds an MA in Applied Theatre from the City University of New York and manages to maintain a thriving career as a professional artist in tandem with his activist and scholarly pursuits. He has been a Fulbright Awardee, an Oregon Shakespeare Festival Producing Fellow and a Scholar in Residence at University of Michigan (Ann Arbor).

Antonio David Lyons is the creator of "We Are Here", a social activism campaign born in South Africa that utilizes discursive play to engage men and boys in themes of identity, masculinity, relationships, gender based violence and HIV/AIDS. We Are Here has implemented programs and toured in South Africa, Namibia and the USA. For more information go to antoniodavidlyons.com.

**********

**Rajendra Ramoon Maharaj** is an Indo-Afro-Caribbean, award-winning, multi-disciplinary, American Theater Artist and Activist. He has been a New York Times Critics Pick and his playwriting residencies include the NOLA Writer's Residency, Alliance Theater, Arkansas Repertory Theater, Milwaukee Repertory Theater, the 2020 Resident Playwright of the LoM Theatre, and is a member of Theater Now's 2021 Virtual Musical Theater Writer's Group.

Mr. Maharaj is a recipient of the 2020 National Alliance for Musical Theater Award. He will be the assistant director in 2021 for Fire Shut Up In My Bones at The Metropolitan Opera. He is a 2021 Season Finalist in The Downtown Urban Arts Festival in New York City, and the inaugural playwright for the Theatre Raleigh New Works Reading Series, winner of the audience choice award and nominated for best play in the inaugural 2021 LGBTQ+ Short Plays Festival, and a semi-finalist in the 2021 Blue Ink Playwriting Award competition presented by American Blues Theater. Mr.

Maharaj is a finalist for the 2021 Eugene O'Neill National Playwrights Conference.

**********

**Marie Mayingi** was born in Paris in 2000 and is currently studying English Law and French Law at the University of Exeter. Her first play, "ANTIGONE" was performed by the Philadelphia Artists' Collective as part of their New Ventures Festival in February 2020. It is also set to be performed by the York College of Pennsylvania and the Crafton Hills College of California as well as B3 Theater's troupe in Summer 2021. Her work was recently chosen to appear in Black Spring Press' "Best New British and Irish Poets 2019-2021" anthology which will be published in June 2021.

**********

**Crystal D. Mayo** is an actress, writer and educator who is a Native New Yorker born and raised in the South Bronx.. Her urban upbringing is a relentless source of inspiration in her writing. Her experiences are highlighted in her upcoming memoir, The Evolution of Me which captures her lifeline of rich and telling childhood recollections told through poetry and prose. Crystal's repertoire of writing spans from memoirs and poetry to children's books. Her literary contributions have been published in the Bronx Memoir Project Volumes three and four, The African Voices tribute to Ntozake Shange and Our Voices Our Stories, an anthology of Writings Advancing, Celebrating, Embracing and Empowering Girls and Women of Color through the National Girls and Women of Council Inc. Crystal holds a masters in elementary education and is the founder and artistic director of My Daughter My Legacy. This entrepreneur's mission statement is to empower youth to discover their voice and vision through literacy and the arts. Crystal teaches students how to write and perform spoken word in addition to creating collaborative performance pieces.

**********

**Maurice Moore** is currently a doctoral Performance Studies Candidate at the University of California-Davis. His creative non-fiction, critical essays, fictional, and visual works have appeared in Existere Journal, bozalta Collective, Harbor Review, Rigorous, Harpy Hybrid Review, Wicked Gay Ways, Storm Cellar Journal, Loud and Queer Zine, Communication and Critical Cultural Studies, Strukturriss Quarterly Journal, HIVES Buzz-Zine, As Loud As It's Kept Magazine, Unlikely Stories Mark V, and Confluence. From 2011 to 2021, he has exhibited work and performed at the Medford Arts Center in New Jersey, Memorial Union Gallery in Fargo North Dakota, the International House Davis (I-House) in Davis California, The Center for Visual Artists in Greensboro North Carolina, Christina Ray Gallery in Soho New York, the Lee Hansley Gallery in Raleigh North Carolina, the Gallery 307 + Orbit Galleries in Athens Georgia, Weatherspoon Art Museum in Greensboro North Carolina, and performed with Rios/Miralda for the Garbage Celebration in Madison Wisconsin. Throughout his career he has been awarded residences at the Penland School of Crafts, Ox-Bow, the Rios/Miralda Garbage Celebration Residency, and the Verge Residency of The Ali Youssefi Project (AYP) at the Verge Center for the Arts in Sacramento California.

**********

**Liz Morgan** is a playwright, poet and performer. Her written work has appeared in The Huffington Post, the Long Island City One Act Festival Anthology and the Medium publication, Athena Talks. She has previously developed projects with The Fire This Time Festival, The Lark, SPACE on Ryder Farm, The Flea, Fresh Ground Pepper, Liberation Theatre Company, Judson Arts, Amios, Rising Circle, JACK, NY Madness, POTPOURRI! World Women Works Series, Rites and Reason Theatre, Manhattan Rep and National Black Theatre where she was named a finalist for the I AM SOUL Playwrights' Residency. Her original plays include her solo show, Deep $h*t, as well as Deliver: Letters to the Motherland from a Foreign Body (2019 Kilroys List Honorable Mention), Breaking & Entering, A Matter of Taste, Our Father and The Clark Doll which was featured at the 2019 Deep Water Literary Festival and nominated for a 2018 Drammy Award in the category of Best Original Script after its west coast premiere. Other honors include the Torchbearer for Black Theatre Award, Playwrights Realm Writing Fellowship (Semi-Finalist) and the New Works Lab at Stratford (Semi-Finalist). MFA: Brown University. LizMorganOnline.com

**********

Born and raised in Chicago's Southside, **Diana Mucci** is an Afro-Latina author, playwright, and producer. She has performed as an actress and has written, published and/or produced short stories, children's books, poems, indie films, and in 2005 her first play, I'm a Female. . . Seeking a Male, which earned accolades from the Chicago Sun-Times. Diana revised the play, now entitled Come 'n Go, and mounted a wildly successful premiere at The Factory Theatre, Chicago in 2018. Diana's credits also include co-producing the indie film, Bloom which premiered at the Chicago Latino Film Festival. She performed a virtual monologue of her short story "Spit" with the esteemed nonprofit A New World of Theater in 2020. She is a member of The Dramatist Guild of America, the Amigos del Rep Council and the Playwright's Collective with A New World of Theater. Diana established Back of the Yards Entertainment in support of diverse artists and is finishing her memoir and one-woman show, Growing up with Big Hair. She lives in the Chicago area with her husband and family.

**********

**K.E. Mullins** is a Jacksonville, Florida native and has enjoyed reading and writing since her early childhood. She began her writing career while in the Navy by venturing into poetry.

Her novel excerpt, "Iben...I've been through some sh@#!" was published in the February 2021 edition of The Write Launch. Additionally, Ms. Mullins' poem, "My One Last Cent," was published in a literary journal, "Amistad" in 2007 at Howard University. She has published a book of poetry, "Thinking Aloud: Dimensions of free-verse" and her fiction series, "The Friends and Family Connection: Get Unplugged", "In the Company of Strangers", and "Murder: Another Name for Revenge" all are available for purchase on Amazon in paperback or Kindle along with her latest novel, "7475 Samona Drive."

In addition to writing poetry, Kimberley has performed at spoken word venues in Urban Grind, Atlanta, GA, Busboys and Poets in Washington, D.C., and the Thomas Center, Gainesville, FL.

**********

**Gladys W. Muturi** was born in Silver Spring, Maryland and currently lives in Germantown, MD. Gladys started acting at the age of eleven in her first play at Montgomery Village Middle School and continued pursuing acting. In the eleventh grade, she entered a Christopher Columbus state essay and won the contest. It became her first writing experience. She has completed two plays: White Mama and A Gathering of Old Men and is currently working on her one act play Boys Like Us.

**********

**Louis DeVaughn Nelson** is an interdisciplinary artist and the founder Hokum Arts started in 2006. Nelson has worked for 20 years as a performer, choreographer, producer and director for film, theater, dance and more. His works have been shown in USA, Europe, Australia and South Korea. He has studied at DeSales University, Drexel University, The New School, The Jeanne Ruddy School of Dance, The Koresh School of Dance, and is a proud member of The Dramatists Guild of America.

Intimate partner violence, racism, sexuality, discrimination, bigotry, misogyny and the marginalization of class and social systems are frequent topics of Nelson's film and dance theater work. His most notable pieces were included in his three-part dance theatre series satirizing sociopolitical warfare and sensationalism in the media in America entitled "Human Error" (2007), "Man Bites Dog" (2010), and "Until Proven Guilty" (2018). In all of these works he used innovative methods combining several media/disciplines - collaborating with photographers, filmmakers, fine artists, and performing artists.

Since the pandemic – he has directed six theatre/dance productions for ZOOM, YouTube, and Twitch with an aim to push the envelope in this time of burgeoning new media.

**********

**T.R. Riggins** is a playwright whose play Otis and Zora produced by Brooklyn's Billie Holiday Theatre garnered several Audelco Award nominations. His solo work, Unbecoming Tragedy: A Ritual Journey Toward Destiny and The Picasso Incident are currently in development. T.R. is also an actor who began his Equity career in the title role of August Wilson's King Hedley II under the direction of the late Israel Hicks for the Denver Center Theatre Company where he was an acting company member. He then went on to play

Stanley and Thorvald, respectively, in the company's adaptation of A Streetcar Named Desire and A Doll's House. He has appeared as Harmond Wilks, Caesar Wilks, and Walter Lee Younger also under the direction of Mr. Hicks, whom he credits along with August Wilson with reawakening his passion for the theatre. This reawakening led to and invigorated his work with New Haven's Collective Consciousness Theatre which include Dr. Martin Luther king Jr. in Katori Hall's The Mountaintop, Lincoln in Suzan Lori Parks' Topdog/Underdog, Kenyatta in Dominique Morisseau's Sunset Baby, and Lucius Jenkins in Jesus Hopped the A Train. T.R. is a also Presidential Scholar Finalist in the Arts.

**********

**Michael Rishawn** is an actor and playwright. New York Credits: *Old Masters* (The Flea), *24-hour plays* (The New School), *History Boys* (Gallery Players), workshops at Roundabout Theatre. Regional: *Handjob* (Echo Theatre) *WigOut* (Studio Theatre), *Much Ado About Nothing, Two Gentleman of Verona, All's Well* (Shakespeare Theatre Co), *A Christmas Carol, Antony & Cleopatra* (Hartford Stage), *Henry V* (Philadelphia Shakespeare). Sundance Screenwriters' Lab Finalist (Mama's Boy), Bay Area Playwrights Festival Finalist (Not Another Sidney Poitier). MFA, UCSD. BFA, The Hartt School.

**********

An award-winning essayist and fiction writer, **J. E. Robinson** is the author of many plays, including "Groove," from which "Monologue for a Tutting Face" was excerpted. His plays have appeared widely. He teaches history at the University of Health Sciences and Pharmacy in St. Louis.

**********

**Alva Rogers**'s writing utilizes magic realism, objects, puppetry, historical characters, and epochs to explore identity and the uses of enchantment. Her most recent play, Roman and Julie, was commissioned by Montalvo Arts Center. During the pandemic, she created an educational web series called Miss Rogers's Wonderful School to support families with children at home. Her play, The Doll Plays, was featured in The Women's Theater Festival (Virtual) lecture on Object Performance in Plays by African American

Women (July 2020). Rogers was a TCG Playwright-in-Residence at The Joseph Papp Public Theater. She has been the recipient of a NY Dance Theatre Workshop Bessie Award, grants from the Rockefeller Foundation, Jim Henson Foundation and New York Foundation for the Arts and residencies at the Eugene O'Neill Theater Center's Puppetry Conference and The Montalvo Arts Center. She has received an MFA (Playwriting) from Brown University, an MFA (Musical Theater Writing) from NYU's Tisch School of the Arts, and an MAT (Teaching History) from Bard College. Ms. Rogers is a member of The Dramatist Guild and SAG/AFTRA. She appears in the films School Daze and Daughters of the Dust among others.

**********

**Gary Earl Ross** is a retired UB professor whose books include The Wheel of Desire, Shimmerville, Blackbird Rising, Beneath the Ice, and the Gideon Rimes mysteries Nickel City Blues, Nickel City Crossfire, and Nickel City Storm Warning (SEG Publishing). His plays have been staged in Buffalo, Rochester, Knoxville, NYC, other U.S. cities, Canada, England, China, India, and Kazakhstan. They include Picture Perfect, Murder Squared, The Scavenger's Daughter, The Mark of Cain, The Guns of Christmas, The Trial of Trayvon Martin, and Matter of Intent, winner of the Edgar Award from Mystery Writers of America. Scheduled productions include Stoker's Guest and Split Wit. Other honors include three Emanuel Fried Outstanding New Play Awards, a LIFT Fiction Fellowship, a Saltonstall Foundation Playwriting Fellowship, an ASI-DEC artist's grant for fiction, and public radio commentary awards from the NY Associated Press and the NY Broadcasters Association. Both The Scavenger's Daughter and Matter of Intent have been adapted into transliterated motion pictures by CITOC Productions of Mumbai, India. Ross is a member of the Just Buffalo Literary Center, Ujima Company Incorporated, the Dramatist Guild, the National Writers Union, and Mystery Writers of America. Visit him at garyearlross.net

**********

A native of Hartford, CT, **Sharece M. Sellem** is a playwright, choreographer, director and performing arts instructor based out of New Haven, CT. She was trained by Headlong Performance

Institute of Bryn Mawr College in Pennsylvania and Yale University's Practical Approach to Directing Summer Program 2014. Her resume includes performances at Bregamos Community Theater, Long Wharf Theatre, Pride Arts Center of Chicago, Charter Oak Cultural Center, Carriage House Theater, Illinois Voices Theatre, Norwich Arts Center, University of California San Diego and more. She is the founder of Vintage Soul Productions LLC.

**********

**Tylie Shider**'s recent plays include *Certain Aspects of Conflict in the Negro Family* (Premiere Stages, 2022), and *The Gospel Woman* (NBT). He is a two-time recipient of the Jerome Fellowship at the Playwrights' Center and an I Am Soul playwright in residence at the National Black Theatre(NBT). He holds a BA in Journalism from Delaware State University and an MFA in Dramatic Writing from NYU. A proud member of the Dramatist Guild, he is currently a Professor of Playwriting at Augsburg University.

**********

**Karen "Magic Fingaz" Smith,** Brooklyn Native, Philly Residence is a Professional Percussionist, Playwright, Poet, Teaching Artist and Curator. Karen is also a receiver of several grants including the Lee Way Foundation, Art and Change and the Pennsylvania Council for Arts for a new musical entitled, "Awoke" opening this Fall . Karen manages two groups, Weez the Peeples and Sistahs Laying Down Hands Collectives. During this shift, new writings, collaborations, recordings and Anthologies were developed; Philly Jawns, For Women Revisited featuring 40 poets as a tribute to Nina Simone and the Phenomenal, 8:46 paying homage to the Life of George Floyd. Possible is Possible is her daily mantra. Website: karensmithdrums.wixsite.com/karensmithdrums
IG: KarenSmithDrums, Facebook Karen Smith

**********

Originally from Lagos, Nigeria, **Kayodè Soyemi** grew up in Atlanta, GA where he fostered his artistic passions. At seven years old, Kayodè began singing and acting, and has since made accomplishments as a writer, designer, producer and director. As an actor he has made appearances at Actor's Express, Dallas Theater Center, Aurora Theatre, Yale Cabaret and Actors Theatre of Louisville. His writing has been been produced at Yale Cabaret, Shaking the Tree, and New World Theatre. Kayodè received his B.F.A. from Meadows School of the Arts at Southern Methodist University and is an alum of the '18-'19 Professional Training Company at Actor's Theatre of Louisville. He is currently pursuing his MFA at Yale School of Drama.

**********

**Christian St. Croix** is an award-winning playwright and the author of "M.", a collection of prose, poetry and micro-fiction that Outword Magazine describes as, "Raw. Real. Radical. Racy."

St. Croix's works include "Princes", winner of the 2017 San Diego International Fringe Festival Award for Outstanding LGBT Performance; "Zack", winner of the Young-Howze Theatre Award for Best Comedic Writing, "And All the Birds Loved Her", an audio play commissioned by Blindspot Collective and the La Jolla Playhouse, and "Monsters of the American Cinema", winner of two 2019 San Diego International Fringe Festival Awards that the San Diego Union-Tribune called "touching and funny", "honest" and "engaging."

He currently resides in San Diego, CA.

**********

**J. J. Tingling** I am the epitome of the information professional. The Author. The Publisher. The Librarian. The Archivist. The Recorder and Witness. I hold words, phrases, letters... in such high regard. Together they build sentences, conversations... whole realms that speak to and tear down the barriers that occupy our physical world. My writings are meant to connect spirits across time and space. To reach a deeper understanding of ourselves and all that is around us in the day. My first collection of poetic work was published in partnership with Ashani Scales in The Brown Female Voice, April of 2020. During a time of great unrest, we hoped our writings would bring comfort, reassurance, and acceptance to our readers. May these words inspire and bolster you. Be well.

**********

**Dr. Mary E. Weems** is a poet, playwright, author, scholar. Weems' earned her B.A. and M.A. from Cleveland State University and her

Ph.D. in Education from the University of Illinois @ Urbana-Champaign. Dr. Weems is the author of thirteen books including Blackeyed: Plays and Monologues and Writings of Healing and Resistance: Empathy and the Imagination-Intellect, five chapbooks, and numerous poems, articles and book chapters. In 2015, Weems' won a Cleveland Arts Prize, and both of her poetry books An Unmistakable Shade of Red and the Obama Chronicles, and For(e)closure, were finalists for Ohioana Book Awards. She's also been nominated for a Pushcart Prize. Her fourteenth book Still Hanging: Using Performance Texts to Deconstruct Racism, co-authored with Dr. Bryant Alexander, is in-press from Brill/Sense Publishers (Spring, 2021) and her fifteenth book with Dr. Bryant Alexander, Collaborative Spirit-Writing and Performance in Everyday Black Lives is forthcoming from Routledge Press. Her monologue "Primary Care," was part of "Intervals" produced by the Dobama Theatre. Her play Crack the Door for Some Air, was just selected for a workshop production by the Big Noise Theatre in Des Plaines, Illinois. To contact Dr. Weems please visit her website at maryeweems.org or email her at maryeweems45@gmail.com

**********

**Bryan-Keyth Wilson** (He, Him, His) Dubbed the Literary Prince, BRYAN-KEYTH WILSON is a noted multi-hyphenate in the theatre and publishing arena. He is a published author of three books, 10 plays, 1 choreopoem and 32 monologues. His first novel, HOOD BOY CHRONICLES, was a groundbreaking work of inspirational fiction combining street lit, and spoken word poetry. Currently BKW has a residency with the Paterson Performing Arts Development Council and is in development of his choreopoem FOR COLORED BOYZ: on the verge of a nervous breakdown/ when freedom ain't enuff. BKW studied Musical Theatre with a Dance emphasis at Sam Houston State University. He serves as the founding artistic director of The Creative Co-Lab TX|NYC. He is now in development of his first comic book series THE TALENTED TENTH on Wilson Comics/ B's Ink Publishing. He is a five-year faculty member of The Black Writers Reunion & Conference and creator of the LIFT EV'RY VOICE International Playwright & Spoken World Virtual Festival. bryankeyth.com IG: @literaryprince

# APPENDIX B — CONTACT INFORMATION

**Nessa Amherst**
(443) 591-7896
neamherst@gmail.com
nessaamherst.com
IG: @nessaamherst

**Melda Beaty**
MeldaCreates, Inc. PO Box 43177 Chicago, IL 60643
melda@meldacreates.com

**Jonathon Benjamin**
jackcodybenjamin@gmail.com
newplayexchange.org/users/21289/jonathon-benjamin

**Mardee Bennett**
Producing organizations may contact Mardee through Amy Wagner of A3 Artists Agency.

**Cris Eli Blak**
crisblakwrites@gmail.com
IG: @criseliblak

**Sharnell Blevins**
sharnellblevins.com

**Sharon Cleveland Blount**
Hersheproductions@gmail.com
PO Box 4837, Valley Village, CA 91617
hersheproductions.com

**Christopher Buchanan**
chris@chrisbuchanan.us

**Cashel Campbell**
Contact@CashelCampbell.com
IG: @layers_of_cash

**Max King Cap**
maxkingcap.com

**Shaneisha Dodson**
st_dodson@yahoo.com

**Vincent Terrell Durham**
Michael Moore Agency
Contact: Samara Harris
450 West 24th Street, Suite 1C, New York, NY 10011
(212) 221-0400
samara@michaelmooreagency.com

**Zachariah Ezer**
zachezer@gmail.com

**Tina Fakhrid-Deen**
shespeaksrivers.com

**LeLand Gantt**
lelandgantt@yahoo.com

**Michael Hagins**
(347) 489-5459
mchagins@gmail.com

**Ardencie Hall-Karambe, PhD**
ardenciehk.ardenblair@gmail.com

**Siri Imani**
facebook.com/siriimaniartistpage
siriimani.com

**James J. Johnson**
JamesJJohnson1@gmail.com

**Louis D. Johnson**
(615) 500-1583 (mobile)
ldelbertj@yahoo.com
newplayexchange.org/users/37011/louis-johnson

**Rachel Lynett**
rachel.lynett@gmail.com

**Antonio David Lyons**
antoniodavidlyons.com

**Rajendra Ramoon Maharaj**
Michael Moore Agency
Contact: Michael Moore
450 West 24th Street, Suite 1C, New York, NY 10011
(212) 221-0400
michael@michaelmooreagency.com

**Marie Mayingi**
mm1014@exeter.ac.uk

**Crystal D. Mayo**
theartistcrystalmayo@gmail.com

**Maurice Moore**
Performance Studies Doctoral Candidate
University of California-Davis
Artmoore@ucdavis.edu
maurice-moore-mkx7.squarespace.com

**Liz Morgan**
liz@lizmorganonline.com

**Diana Mucci**
dimucci66@gmail.com

**K.E. Mullins**
(352) 246-0917
kimberley.mullins@outook.com
TWITTER: K.E.Mullins@jazypoet

**Gladys W. Muturi**
pop.princess63@gmail.com
IG: @gladys_muturi95

**Louis DeVaughn Nelson**
thehokumarts@gmail.com

**T.R. Riggins**
CHI Talent Management
(917) 769-6009 (c)

**Michael Rishawn**
michaelrishawn@gmail.com
IG: @michaelrishawn

**J. E. Robinson**
jerobinson1008@gmail.com

**Alva Rogers**
IG: @alvasworld
alvasworld.com

**Gary Earl Ross**
geross@buffalo.edu

**Sharece M. Sellem**
smsellem@vintagesoulproductions.com
VintageSoulProductions.com

**Tylie Shider**
trs347@nyu.edu

**Karen L Smith**
karensmithdrums.wixsite.com/karensmithdrums

**Kayodè Soyemi**
kayode.shxw@gmail.com

**Christian St. Croix"**
saintsriot@gmail.com
saintscrossing.com

**J. J. Tingling**
J&B Press LLC
900 N. 19th Street #3242, Philadelphia, PA 19130
215-495-2900
jandbpressphilly@gmail.com

**Dr. Mary E. Weems**
maryeweems45@gmail.com
maryeweems.org

**Bryan-Keyth Wilson**
Alexandria C. Scott, ESQ
Info@legallymarked.com
(281) 624-5854

Made in the USA
Middletown, DE
20 June 2021

42797392R00089